Labor of God

Labor of God
The Agony of the Cross as the Birth of the Church

Thomas Andrew Bennett

BAYLOR UNIVERSITY PRESS

Jacket design by Rebecca Lown
Jacket image: Depiction of the church emerging from the side of the
crucified Christ, from *Bible moralisée: Codex Vindobonensis 2554*,
Vienna, sterreichischen Nationalbibliothek commentary and translation
of biblical texts by Gerald B. Guest. Image courtesy of the holdings of
Special Collections & University Archives, UCR Library, University of
California, Riverside, call number ND3355.V5213 1995.

This book has been catalogued by the Library of Congress with the
ISBN 978-1-4813-0649-2.

Printed in the United States of America on acid-free paper with a
minimum of 30 percent postconsumer waste recycled content.

CONTENTS

Acknowledgments   vii

1   Retrieving the Forgotten Root   1
The Scandal of the Cross as the Labor of God

2   Speaking the Labor of God   17
Metaphor and the Truth of Religious Language

3   Converting the Cross   39
How Torture Becomes Childbirth

4   Birthing the Church   61
How the Cross Addresses Sin

5   Transcending Exchange   77
How the Family of God Gives Up the Gift

6   Expanding the Agony of the Cross   89
How Labor Opens Fresh Theological Frontiers

Notes   105
Bibliography   127
Scripture Index   141
Subject Index   143

ACKNOWLEDGMENTS

This project was in its early stages before my wife, Erin, gave birth to our first daughter, Alice, but that event was what made the academic personal. Before Alice, the cross as the labor of God was a neat idea, a new way to think about atonement and perhaps some other theological issues. But the blood and water Erin gave to bring Alice into the world drew what was just an idea out of the abstract and incarnated it. In memory, Erin's labor is—to me, at least—a blur, yet somehow precisely etched, indistinct in the particulars but pristinely captured, like how Monet pictures a bridge spanning a pond of water lilies. If the Scriptures and the Christian tradition have depicted the cross of Christ as something like this, it seemed, then surely the atonement of God revealed a hideous kind of beauty. For now there was for me no question either of birth's majesty or of its horror. Childbirth—whether divine or human—is a reckoning. It is radical. So, therefore, should be the church's annunciation. Truly it was with Alice that this book was born.

Along the way, numerous friends and colleagues have challenged and counseled and cheered the labor of God. Murray Rae's sparkling essay in *IJST* inspired this project and furnished tantalizing hints about what fresh theological nuggets labor might help unearth. Alan Padgett's philosophical acumen provided much needed conceptual rigor. Nancey Murphy saw me as a writer and worked to shape me as such; I trust she is not terribly disappointed with the return on her investment. Joel B. Green gave the labor of God encouragement and conceptual space to grow, always pushing me to blend and interweave strands from biblical studies, theology, the sciences, and philosophy—to interpret Scripture theologically, carefully, and yet with curious, passionate abandon. While he is mostly relegated to the notes here, John Goldingay lurks behind most every line I write in one way or another. It was in his home that I began to relearn the art of reading the Bible; I trust he won't be too bothered where I've departed from his methods and sensibilities.

I am deeply grateful to Carey Newman and the incredible people at Baylor University Press for believing in this book and dedicating countless hours and ideas to it. Carey is by turns frightening, inspiring, entertaining, and overwhelming. If any surplus of his charisma has spilled onto these pages, I will be sincerely gratified.

It strikes me that the book you are about to read is almost unrecognizable from the version that Carey originally plopped into Jordan Rowan Fannin's lap. And it further strikes me that she probably saw its heart before I did, distracted as I was by defensive notes, protracted arguments, and the minutiae of academic discourse. She spent time with it and saw past its cold exterior; she read between and behind the lines and saw the passion that academic pretension had in many ways suppressed. So if you find yourself in any way recaptured or maybe even enraptured by the dark glory of the cross as you read, you will want to thank Jordan. She coaxed that prose out of me, pressed me to find it and seize it because she believed it mattered and was worth doing. Her tireless and frankly stunning editorial efforts have brought clarity, energy, and drive to the many places where my own work was muddled and desultory. If this book is an infant, Jordan was co-parent to the pregnancy: we have labored together, stretching and pushing all the way to bring this baby to term, and I hope she is as proud and beaming a parent as I am.

My family—both by blood at home and by Spirit at Coast Bible Church—has been unreasonably patient and, not to put too fine a point on it, overly indulgent, affording me the time and space to read and write in the midst of being a husband, father, son, pastor, and teacher. Some, like Jack Kulp, have made it financially possible. Others, like my friends Jeani Toscano, Colleen Varela, John Mitchell, and David Eichner, as well as my parents David and Joyce Bennett, have encouraged me to put other things aside and keep at it but also to take a break and surf when it was most needed.

My deepest thanks go to Erin Christine, my best friend and partner, my greatest love, and the indefatigable mother of Alice and Olivia. She, like no other woman I know, models herself after Mother Jesus, and Erin's labor—like the Lord's—is never in vain.

1

RETRIEVING THE FORGOTTEN ROOT
The Scandal of the Cross as the Labor of God

How strange that the career of Jesus of Nazareth, defined as it is by his being tortured to death for blasphemy and sedition, is apparently an offense to no one, especially his followers. This really is extraordinary; Christians have become utterly inured to the cross—an instrument of humiliation and cruelty—as a religious symbol. Having stripped it of any intimation of scandal, having sanitized it, having rendered it inert and anodyne, the language Christians use of the cross as ransom, sacrifice, victory, and so forth has lost much of its essence. To put the problem simply, though we will presently complicate it at length, traditional Christian speech about the cross has become toothless through long repetition, such that it no longer truly points to the thing it is meant to explain. This should be plain: Christianity—a religion whose primary symbol is an offense bordering on grotesquerie—is by turns irrelevant and anesthetizing. The church's proclamation of the cross has lost the essence of the proclamation of the cross. For the cross' essence is in part comprised of its radicality, that God has effected ultimate change in lives and in the world in this way and not some other.

How very strange then that familiarity with Christian speech about the cross precludes Christians from thinking the cross radical at all. It is as if making sense of Jesus' crucifixion—as sacrifice or debt payment or exchange or spiritual victory—itself robs the cross of something of its dark splendor, or masks, hides, or defers something of its sensationalism. For "making sense" is what the atonement metaphors are meant to do. They redescribe a senseless, unjust murder as salvation, hope, and peace. This treads close to paradox: many were crucified by the Roman Empire, but only one man's crucifixion is taken to have changed the world. And only by redescribing that crucifixion as something that is not simply crucifixion can Christians give substantive content or meaning to that claim. And yet the redescriptions—the very vehicle by which Christian language confronts the world with God's scandalous rescue-by-cross—were apparently predestined to lose the heart of what they were minted to communicate.

There is a way, however, to seize again the radicality of the message of the cross. A way to reinvigorate the theology of the cross—that is, atonement theology—without resorting to cheap bombast or sloganeering. There is, in fact, a way to deepen our knowledge of the cross' radicality as never before. A new configuration of the cross that faithfully invites a deeper understanding of God's nature and of what God was doing with the cross is possible. It is to more faithfully reckon God's agency in the death of an innocent prophet. It is not only to be awed once again by the visceral nature of liberation-by-execution but to rereckon its violence, to reinvestigate its purpose, to see in it a new logic, even a new telos.

This new way forward is not, however, linguistic or conceptual innovation. Twenty-first-century first-world human ingenuity is doubtless of great value in many of the sciences but not in a theology of the cross. How could it be? What do modern, educated people know of the death of Nazarene peasants at imperial whim? Academic theologians are, if anything, more likely to be brandishing the sword of the empire than pricked on its point. There is therefore a problem of location. To recapture the essence of the cross, one must be close enough to it socially and spiritually to be able to embrace it and become its offense, to perpetuate its scandal. These are not domains within which contemporary scholarship typically wanders. To put it plainly, it is not enough simply to conjure up a new image for Jesus' crucifixion and place it above the storied metaphors of the tradition. Such an act of hubris could not possibly be adequate to the task of revitalizing the essence of what is, above all else, a humble, humiliating death.

Nor is a fresh theology of the cross to be found by retracing steps in well-worn paths, supposing that surely this time some new nook or cranny will be exposed, some vital stone found that is worth overturning. What has already been said of the cross has already been said of the cross. The cross is a "sacrifice," yes, but no further consideration of that image will make it any less staid, proper, stale, and dead. And this is not at all to say that the cross is not a sacrifice. It is, rather, to say that a theology of the cross predicated on the centrality of that description will fail to articulate properly its meaning. It may actually fail to expose rightly the nature and character of God, and this not because calling Jesus' crucifixion a sacrifice is somehow inherently misleading; on the contrary, when first Christians deployed this language, they truly expressed truth and power. We know this because the world was changed by the message they carried. The radical nature of the claim remained intact; the cross' description was suitably and simultaneously gracious and offensive, and so the world and its inhabitants were altered through the Word of the Lord. But this event cannot be repeated. Or, rather, it has been repeated with such numbing fidelity that the effect—the change—no longer follows the transmission.

The theology of the cross cannot exist without the Bible. Indeed, the atonement and the Bible are inseparable. A fresh iteration of the meaning of the cross is not so much extracted from the Scriptures, however, as found by thinking with them. This is worth fleshing out. Traditionally, theology has made sense of the cross by locating this or that image in the works of, say, Paul and supplying a kind of internal logic by which the image could be mapped onto a narrative or conceptual scheme. So if Paul calls the cross a "ransom," then the scholar searches high and low in order to detect who was ransomed from whom, with what, and for how much. There is value in this work, but it is, as we have already suggested, tired, bloodless. New insights into the nature of the God of the cross emerge not by textual interrogation as traditionally practiced but instead by a kind of thinking that moves *with* the grains of texts. Theology can do better than merely appropriating or reappropriating Paul's argot. But this is not the same thing as saying that it can do without Paul (or James or Ezekiel, etc.). Recapturing the glory and the shame of the cross, being once again jarred and converted by it, does not leave the Bible behind but rather interacts with it in creative and surprising ways.

The *teologia crucis* that remains true to the essence of the nature of the cross is discovered in the overlooked interstices of the language of the Christian tradition. Christian theology has, like a poplar's roots, expanded in many directions over the millennia, growing by fits and starts in the ongoing attempt to reckon God, Scripture, the cross, and human life and culture. It is not unreasonable to assume that at least a few of these conceptual tendrils have been unfairly or prematurely abandoned and that a root that should have grown and deepened perhaps did not, leaving the tree unexpectedly fragile as a result.

Among these tendrils and roots, there is one image in particular that has cropped up from time to time, in the thoughts and writings of mystics and anchoresses, church fathers and mothers. It is an image of the cross that burst forth in visions and was then abruptly dropped, left by the wayside in systematic, doctrinal work. Perhaps the implications of this way of framing cross-thought were simply too radical—if such a thing is even possible—for theology to comprehend. Like classical Pauline images of the cross, it is strange and unruly, picturing the cross—surely the paradigmatic expression of despair—as surprisingly hopeful. Like the image of sacrifice it does not shrink from crucifixion's physical horror, but unlike sacrifice it does not trade in the conceptual economy of victims and perpetrators. It eschews, in fact, notions of economy entirely, radically opposing the cross to the language of exchange, of this for that, him for us. And yet it does so without losing the concept of cost, of the truth that whatever Jesus' crucifixion accomplished, it did so only at great physical, emotional, and psychological cost to the man Jesus and, possibly, the implicated Godhead. Like the image of victory, this overlooked metaphor, this biblical but not merely exegetical image, this ignored root from the Christian tradition, pictures the cross as embodied, costly exertion that succeeds. But the victory embedded in it is different from classical articulations of *Christus Victor*, for this fresh vision of the cross does not picture invisible forces or spiritual adversaries as the agents of our oppression. It instead remembers in the best Christian way that it is ultimately the corrupting influence of sin that must be defeated, and it makes sense of how the cross can actually do this.

This image, the one that really can revivify a *teologia crucis* for the twenty-first century, ultimately draws its power from a deep connection to genesis, that is, origination. It evokes a semantic field that encompasses growth, new life, a fresh start, and the rhythms of the known, observable universe wherein pain and sometimes death are the fertilizers out of which new life springs. And this is how it accounts for the change that Christians confess the cross brings to persons, communities, and even the world itself. It is able to conceptualize coherently an instrument of denigration and torture as the process or mechanism out of which newness comes, new life for people as well as their environs.

In this largely unnoticed strand of Christian theology, the crucifixion of Jesus of Nazareth is known as the birthing pangs—the labor—of God, who bears renewed, spiritual sons and daughters into the world. The blood and water that poured from Jesus are the blood and water that have accompanied every infant that has entered the world. The scarring harm, unavoidable and intrinsic to birth, marked too the body of the incarnate, laboring God. New life and new hope, long the prize and purpose of labor, spring forth in the Spirit from the mothering Jesus, incarnating into a dying world spiritual sons and daughters, possessors of God's own inextinguishable life and heritable character. The cross is the labor of God. And in theological reflection drawn from this image, we argue that contemporary Christian atonement theology may once again recover the brazen, dissonant, radically gracious self-giving love of God.

Recovering a Discarded Image: The Cross as the Labor of God

The image of the cross of Christ as God's labor to bring about spiritual birth emerges from Scripture, specifically the Gospel of John and elsewhere in Johannine literature, and is taken up—usually inchoately—at the edges of the Christian theological tradition. In modern scholarship it surfaces occasionally, often in feminist biblical and theological work. It is certainly not novel, in any case. And yet, because it has lingered outside the major streams of Christian reflection on the theology of the cross, it has retained the theological potential to communicate freshly the harsh beauty of God's nature and saving character: "theological potential," because biblical scholars and systematic and constructive theologians have largely neglected to take such imagery seriously as a reliable guide in ongoing theological reflection. So it is that in what follows I will show how the Gospel of John promulgates the image but never examines it, that John instead jumps forward to articulate the end result of labor, namely divine parentage for those born. In the poems and prayers and visions of the primarily medieval tradition, the language of motherhood and labor teases a theology of the cross but never explicates it; salvific renewal and world-generation are in view but, conceptually speaking, out of focus. Modern theology fares a bit better, especially in recent decades, but again, there is little in the way of sustained, rigorous reflection on the question of what it means that the crucifixion at Golgotha is the scene of spiritual birth. Nevertheless, these exegetical and theological insights form the conceptual material out of which a vital—that is, renewed and compelling—*teologia crucis* is formed.

The Labor of God in Scripture, the Tradition, and Modern Theology

In the mid-to-late 1980s and early 1990s, a spate of North American studies appeared that paid particular attention to the New Testament's new or second birth language. Reading between the lines, we get the sense that scholars were finally weighing in on the then recent American phenomenon of "born again" experiences in evangelical lay theology. So Beverly Roberts Gaventa laments that in "contemporary usage, to be 'born again' refers most often to the experience of an individual."[1] Gaventa then goes on to demonstrate that in, for example, Johannine usage, being "born from above" involves embeddedness into a conversion community.[2] William Orr and William Guy begin their study observing, "From the currency of the term 'born again,' and from the reported frequency of 'born again' experiences, one would expect to find copious [examples in the New Testament]."[3] A subsequent word search subverts this expectation, and in what follows Orr and Guy spend considerable time arguing that the New Testament is more interested in a divine birth or "birth from above" than in being "born again." One suspects that they are animated by popular usage of the term and have put some stock in the task of altering the diction of public discourse. This is worth noting for two reasons. First, one would be hard-pressed to suggest that "birth from above" is not also a second birth.[4] Both phrases are metaphorical, and, as we will see, though "birth from above" language more properly captures the literary and narratival sense of the Fourth Gospel, if γεννηθῇ ἄνωθεν ("born again/anew/from above"; John 3:3, 7) is related theologically to ἀναγεγεννημένοι ("born anew"; 1 Peter 1:23) or παλιγγενεσίας ("renewal," "rebirth"; Titus 3:5), then differences in articulation might fall by the wayside. Either way, if we have already been physically born, then surely a "birth from above" would indeed constitute being "born again." The second reason for highlighting the apparent motives behind earlier studies is that doing so helps us avoid mere repetition of others' hard-won conclusions and, on occasion, helps us steer clear of inferences drawn at least as much from a popular agenda as the sway of the actual evidence.

As has been hinted at already, much exegetical ink has been spilled over the translation of γεννηθῇ ἄνωθεν. The NIV reads the popular "born again," the NRSV follows the majority of scholars with "born from above,"[5] and the CEB, mirroring Gaventa's suggestion, reads "born anew." The problem arises out of an ambiguity in Greek that English speakers do not share. The word ἄνωθεν can indicate either something happening a second time (Galatians 4:9) or something coming "from above" (James 1:17).[6] As most commentators have noted, understanding John's telling of the episode depends on recognizing that Nicodemus is mistaken in how he interprets what Jesus is saying. In the first place, he has substituted the meaning "again" for the meaning "from above." By itself, this mistake only demands clarification to be rectified since being born from above is in fact a species of second birth. Nicodemus' second mistake, however, is more revealing. He does not intuit that Jesus is speaking metaphorically. It is therefore critical that Jesus' response to Nicodemus' quip about entering the womb a second time doubles down on the use of metaphor. Jesus responds to Nicodemus' misunderstanding by saying, "No one can enter the kingdom of God without *being born of water and Spirit*" (John 3:5). Instead of producing a substitute for the birth metaphor, Jesus reinforces it while also reinscribing its literality. Rather than reducing "born" to something like "sharing in," "receiving," or "possessing," the clarification, as it were, glosses "from above" with "water and Spirit"—heightening rather than diminishing the seriousness of Nicodemus' reply. Notice that this is not always Jesus' practice when speaking of the Spirit. When Jesus encourages believers to "drink" him, the metaphor is subsequently replaced with something much more literal:

> On the last day of the festival, the great day, while Jesus was standing there, he cried out, "Let anyone who is thirsty come to me, and let the one who believes in me drink. As the scripture has said, 'Out of the believer's heart shall flow rivers of living

water.'" Now he said this about the Spirit, which believers in
him were to receive; for as yet there was no Spirit, because Jesus
was not yet glorified. (John 7:37-39 NRSV)

When the Spirit comes, believers are to "drink" (πινέτω), that is,
"receive" (λαμβάνειν). What is narrated here is a straightforward case
of a metaphor susceptible to substitution. Where we see "water" we
replace it with "Spirit," and where we see "drink" we replace it with
"receive." The poetic language is mere ornament; Jesus' proclamation
can be restated with less metaphorical terminology.[7]

The language of second birth is therefore suggestive; it hints at
theological depths in a way that other metaphors in John do not. It is
enigmatic, forcing us to ask, "What is birth from above for John? What
does it signal?" In short, "birth from above" takes place in Jesus' crucifixion, and it signals the process by which human beings become natural children of God. In and through the cross, a fundamental change
takes place in the relations holding between human beings, Jesus, and
the Father—and the change implicates family and, in twenty-first century terms, DNA. At the cross, Jesus labors to bring humanity into
God's family. He gives us our second birth. Further exegetical work
bears out such a reading.

In John 20, the resurrected Jesus appears to and commissions
Mary Magdalene. He asks her to tell "his brothers" (ἀδελφούς μου), "I
am ascending to my Father and your Father, to my God and your God"
(20:17b). In these, the first missional words of the post-resurrection
Christ in John's Gospel, two important changes have taken place. First,
"my brothers" refers—as we discover when Mary delivers the message—to the disciples and not to Jesus' blood relations. This is a new
development because previously the disciples and Jesus' family were
differentiated: the disciples "believed in him" (2:11), and his actual
brothers did not (7:5).[8] Jesus' family appears to have expanded or perhaps changed entirely. His disciples have become brothers, either joining or supplanting his brothers by human birth. The second change is
related to the first. For the first time in John's Gospel, God is known as
"Father" to someone other than Jesus. Ramsey Michaels emphasizes
the significance of the change: "This is a milestone in the Gospel, for it
is the first and only instance (out of 120 in all!) in which God is explicitly identified as 'Father' of anyone except Jesus himself."[9] It is as if
the disciples have been traversing levels of familiarity with Jesus, first

following, then becoming friends (15:14-15), then in one case sharing his mother (19:27), and now, after his resurrection, becoming a part of his immediate family. They share his parentage and now relate to him as they relate to one another, as brothers and sisters.

They have, as John says elsewhere, been born from above; they have been born a second time. Thus, it is that the cross has been the labor of God to bring us, God's spiritual children, to birth. And as Teresa Okure observes, "This birth is brought about by Jesus's passion, death and resurrection. Jesus gave birth to believers on the cross (cf. 12:20; 16:21), through his pierced side whence blood and water gushed out as happens to a woman's womb when she gives birth to a child."[10] Since the Fourth Gospel frequently associates water and blood with life and the Spirit, the birth from above of John 3 fits conceptually with John's narration of the cross.[11] These claims are at once exegetical and theological, taking into account both the language of John's Gospel and the theological interpretation of the tradition.[12]

The tradition of the church has not been voluble in promoting this view, but neither has it been silent. In a prayer to St. Paul, St. Anselm appends an aside directly to the Lord Jesus:

> You have died more than they, that they may labour to bear.
> It is by your death that they have been born,
> for if you had not been in labour,
> you could not have borne death;
> and if you had not died, you would not have brought forth.
> For, longing to bear sons into life,
> you tasted of death,
> and by dying you begot them.[13]

Anselm specifically cites the passion as the event of our birth by Mother Jesus, equating the suffering-unto-death of the cross with maternal labor. Jesus' death brings life to spiritual children. Notice, however, how atonement is connected not only to death but to the labor pains themselves. Jesus' bearing the death of humanity requires labor, Anselm thinks. When contextualized within his larger satisfaction scheme, it may be that Anselm is recognizing Jesus' willingness to "take the cup," as it were, as constitutive of achieving eternal benefits for human beings. But in the linguistic world of the prayer, where Anselm invokes the labor metaphor, he makes the logical connection demanded by the human experience of childbirth: new life is necessarily precipitated by the pains of labor. Anselm therefore anticipates something of the nature of our present work, in which taking the labor metaphor seriously provides a conceptual entrée into systematic theology. Anselm's theology of satisfaction interacts with the image of childbirth; it is difficult to say to what extent this intermingling leaves either satisfaction theory or the labor metaphor changed—it takes place, after all, in the midst of a poetic prayer to St. Paul—but the conceptual possibilities are nevertheless there. The labor of God has the potential to teach new truths about labor and about God.

Julian of Norwich echoes the same themes of pain and birth:

> But our true Mother Jesus, he alone bears us for joy and for endless life, blessed may he be. So he carries us within him in love and travail, until the full time when he wanted to suffer the sharpest thorns and cruel pains that ever were or will be, and at the last he died. And when he had finished, and had borne us so for bliss, still all this could not satisfy his wonderful love.[14]

The language of labor pains is explicit, as is the connection between those pains and human beings receiving some sort of salvation in which we are "borne to bliss" or to "joy and endless life." The sufferings of the cross produce life; we are the children, and Christ is the mother who dies to give us birth. In the world conjured by Julian's language we may even be invited to think of Jesus' life and ministry as a pregnancy, such that he "carries us within him in love and travail." Such language is at once shocking and theologically suggestive, reframing the gospel narrative in such a way that, like a woman bringing a child to term, Jesus' ministry is telescoped and his labor on the cross pictured as its telos. In Julian we now know the Only Begotten as True Begetter, wherein the Son of the Father's life, ministry, and death mothers the church. Julian is quick to connect the "sharpest thorns"—that is, crucifixion nails—with the pangs of labor, reminding us that Jesus mothers as human mothers do: in travail. Another theologian from the medieval period, Marguerite d'Oingt, also connects Jesus, labor, and salvation-through-birth:

> Oh, sweet and lovely Lord, how bitterly were you in labor for me all through your life! But when the time approached where you had to give birth, the labor was such that your holy sweat

was like drops of blood which poured out of your body onto the ground. . . . Oh, Sweet Lord Jesus Christ, who ever saw any mother suffer such a birth! But when the hour of the birth came you were placed on the hard bed of the cross where you could not move or turn around or stretch your limbs as someone who suffers such great pain should be able to do. . . . And surely it was no wonder that your veins were broken when you gave birth to the world all in one day.[15]

This is still the language of medieval popular piety, when speech about "Mother Jesus" was widespread.[16] Marguerite, like Julian and Anselm, departs from regular usage, however, by specifying the actual "birthing" that takes place at the cross and possibly connects this with first creation, indicating that God's creative activity in Genesis, completed through the Son, proceeded through the Son's mothering labor. The labor image is a strange one, of course, because Jesus was, in fact, male; it is difficult to envisage the mechanics, so to speak, of spiritual birth. For her part, Marguerite explicitly references the bloodletting Jesus experienced on the cross, which likely implicates the wound in his side. Interestingly, a thirteenth-century French Moralized Bible contains images depicting the church emerging from the wound in Jesus' side while he remains affixed to the cross.[17] In conjunction with the salvific overtones in Anselm and the implication of Jesus' life and ministry as pregnancy in Julian, we have in medieval piety something like a metaphorical model of the spiritual birth of Christians and thereby the church, located in and through the incarnate life of the Son. In a way, this image functions as a reconceptualization of the birth theme in the Fourth Gospel: though birth from above is not here mapped out in systematic or constructive terms, it at least draws out some of the narratival implications of John's proclamation that the Word became flesh and lived among us.

Anselm's poem, Julian's revelation, the illustration of the birth of the church, and Marguerite's affective vision all indicate that medieval treatment of Jesus' labor pains assumed that labor implicates atonement, for in each case some mention is made of the generation or salvation of human beings. Other medieval conceptions of Mother Jesus tended to focus on Jesus' maternal nature more in terms of nurturing or teaching; similarly, the tradition received from the church fathers nods to the image of feeding on the Eucharist from Christ's breast.[18] Maternal imagery along these lines is found in Origen, Irenaeus, John

Chrysostom, Ambrose, and Augustine and, as near contemporaries to the medieval writers we have already reviewed, Bernard of Clairvaux, Peter Lombard, Thomas Aquinas, and Bonaventure as well.[19] The juxtaposition of labor and the cross, however, speaks directly to the role of the cross in putting to rights the human condition in such a way as to produce new spiritual life.

It is worth noting, however, that Jesus' motherhood, richly attested in both the Scriptures and the tradition, is untreated systematically. We have a fragment in a poem by Anselm, or a pietistic paean in Julian or Marguerite, but never a substantive theological treatise. Anselm pens *Cur Deus Homo* but passes on *Cur Deus Mater*. Perhaps Mother Jesus' labor on the cross has been thought or felt too scandalous. Alternatively, perhaps the timing was not yet right. Certainly in Anselm's day the language of sacrifice and substitution had yet to be exhausted; the substance of his atonement theology is just the fleshing out of what classical metaphors might mean. His argument in *Cur Deus Homo* by turns startles, fascinates, and compels Boso, the interlocutor. And for good reason: neither Boso nor anyone else had heard the incarnation and the cross preached in this way before. Anselm's gospel simultaneously offends and attracts Boso, laying infinite debt and infinite benefit at his feet in an unprecedented articulation of honor, humiliation, and the gracious interpolation of the God-human between God and humans. It might be the case that, in the premodern era, Christian theology did not yet need to be reawakened, braced by the image and implications of the cross as labor and birth. There are signs, however, that what may have been theologically premature in the medieval era is now approaching—to borrow Julian's phrase—its full time.

So it is that the labor metaphor has enjoyed something of a renaissance in the wake of recent attention to maternal language in medieval piety. Many feminist readers have noted the challenge Jesus' motherhood poses to societal notions of male superiority. Praying to Jesus as Mother forces recognition that "the maleness of Jesus is quite accidental to his meaning as Christ," since, presumably, the salvific act of crucifixion was primarily an act of birth.[20] Others go further, arguing that Jesus' maternal nature is what makes him palatable as savior even in the midst of feminist critiques.[21] Some feminist theorists use birth-at-the-cross imagery to contextualize their own sufferings in childbirth, offering a modern take on affective reflection on the metaphor.[22] The labor of human mothers today—and especially of those without access to modern medical care—is itself an incarnation of Jesus' salvific ministry to the world. One advantage to reading the cross through the lens of personal labor and the subsequent work of childrearing has been attention to the role of the woman such that generativity, rather than sacrifice, marks her role.[23] Accordingly, Jesus' labor on the cross should be hailed not for the grisly nature of his death but for its productivity. In fact, it is Jesus' love for life that ought to norm Christian ethics. Feminist theologians who sound similar notes can caution feminist readers against "reading for productive pain in tales of crucifixion," recommending instead the conviction that Jesus identifies with those for whom "birth [is] at the threshold of death and whose outcome is uncertain."[24]

It is not only theologians—feminist theologians in particular—who have taken up the theme of the cross as labor. A number of biblical scholars have noted exegetical echoes and intimations of the cross as Christ's labor in New Testament texts.[25] For example, it might be that the pregnant and laboring woman of Revelation 12:2 is actually a veiled reference to Jesus on the cross.[26] If this is indeed the case, then it might also be that the image Jesus uses in John 16:21 of a woman's labor pain being no longer remembered after the birth has, if not a double reference, then at least a strong association with the pain of the cross.[27]

Murray Rae augments this storied tradition by taking an additional conceptual step. Rather than simply marshaling references to the labor of God from the tradition and remarking—as we have above—on the clear connection between birth and atonement, Rae suggests that the metaphor might possess systematic or constructive theological currency. "The metaphor of travail," he writes, "thus holds together creation and redemption. The work of redemption is not separate from the work of creation; rather it completes that work by providing the conditions for participation in the new life of communion with God according to his intention."[28] The statement is remarkable in two respects. First, Rae makes the logical connection between new spiritual birth and cosmic creation, a connection upon which we will capitalize and expand throughout this study, for surely the election of Israel and eschatological redemption also involve creation and new life and are perhaps themselves examples of birth from above.

The second—and perhaps more important—aspect of his insight— is his unstated assumption that the labor metaphor offers us some epistemic access into Christian theology. Sophisticated readings of medieval mother, birth, and labor language already demonstrate that this extended image has within it the same theological potential as those images with which the church has become so familiar—sacrifice, ransom, victory, and so forth. Labor is not, we hasten to clarify, a cipher for some other view of atonement, nor is it poetic ornament suitable only for literary and, subsequently, ethical effect. If we envisage, for example, the water and blood from Jesus' side as Christ's labor with the Spirit, we may have something new to say about the vivification brought economically by the life-giving Spirit.[29] In John 7:39, water—perhaps prefiguring the water and blood that pour from Jesus' side—is the Spirit believers will receive once the Spirit has come into the world. Labor is thus not a metaphor that is meant to be left alone. It rather cries out for serious handling as it promises to offer fresh insights into God's economy and even God's being. The present study aims to capitalize on some of this promise, offering the deep biblical and theological reflection through which the labor of God offers a way to address thorny issues related to the cross in Christian theology.

In light of academic theology's relatively recent rediscovery of the cross as labor and Jesus as mother, and given the alarming inefficacy of tired recitations of the cross as sacrifice or substitution or ransom, it is time for theology to embrace the language of Scripture and tradition and see where a theology of the cross as the labor of God might take us. If an essential feature of a faithful proclamation of the cross is radicality, then we may expect to shock and be shocked as Mother Jesus and the labor of God reconfigure what the church teaches about reconciliation in and through a humiliating death. We may also expect that said shocks will reverberate throughout our doctrinal commitments. Of course Christology—but also impassibility, creation, necessity, and even pneumatology and the divine processions—will all be subject to revitalization and reconfiguration in light of the labor of the mothering God. It is therefore the privilege of the present moment to flesh out the conceptual potential of the image of the cross as labor, that it might revivify Christian proclamation of the Gospel, recapturing its radicality and thus returning it to its essence as the shockingly violent story of God's spiritual and cosmic generation of life.

With this metaphor—drawn as it is from Scripture, the tradition, and contemporary theological reflection—as a guide, theology stands poised to offer fresh insights into long-standing aporias in atonement thought as well as concomitant contributions to Christian construals of the nature of God and the universe. A theology of the cross as labor will therefore speak first to redemption but then point beyond this narrower field to the full panoply of Christian theology as such. And while what is on offer here is not a comprehensive systematic theology with the labor metaphor at its heart, this project nevertheless generates suggestive, constructive proposals along the way.

2

SPEAKING THE LABOR OF GOD
Metaphor and the Truth of Religious Language

Something essential has been lost in the Christian proclamation of the cross and the way it reconciles God and humanity. Such a claim will, in some quarters, be blasé at best and cliché at worst as ministers and evangelists see fewer and fewer lives transformed by an encounter with the gospel even when swathes of people seem at least tacitly to assent to the content of the message. No doubt there is an intuitive pull in the claim that this is because atonement theology has become worn out from repetition, but it is worth analyzing this claim from a philosophical perspective for two reasons that are, in the end, two sides of the same coin. First, it will be helpful to understand how and why metaphors die, why they lose their currency, how they are transformed from purveyances of timely, shocking truths into a patois so inert as to be unnoticed. On the flip side of such an analysis is an account of why seeing the cross as the labor of God can, in current contexts, recapture the vitality of classical language, both reconnoitering undiscovered conceptual space—thus truthfully speaking about the nature and character of the triune God—and remaining faithful to the longstanding trajectories of orthodox faith. In short, we need to know that atonement theology can actually be saved, as it were, and that the proclamation of the cross can in fact be fresh, jarring, and radical without detouring into untruth.

Contemporary philosophy of religious language grew out of the dry, oft-times hostile ground afforded by the philosophical climate at the twilight of the modern era. In the age of Bertrand Russell, mathematics (accompanied by her handmaiden, physics) was crowned queen of the academic sciences[1] and the philosophic-linguistic result—logical positivism—was, to say the least, skeptical of the possibility that religious language could successfully refer, in general, to the numinous and, in particular, to God. Grounded in a thoroughgoing empiricism, logical positivists claimed that the vast majority of human language is merely ornamental and that in the final analysis all meaningful statements can (and perhaps should) be reduced to empirically verifiable claims. In its more strident forms, the introduction of a "verification principle" meant that all metaphysics—including, of course, theological discourse—was to be eliminated.[2] These were the days when acceptance of the methodologies of the natural sciences remained mostly unmarred by conceptual fallout from works that examined the actual practice of empiricism and demonstrated that whatever lofty claims were being made about the nature of scientific research and its drive toward the truth, the evidence quite emphatically disagreed.[3] As such, the primary task of the philosopher of religious language, supposing of course that she were seeking in some way to offer her subject validation, was apologetic.[4] This was in some ways blinding, for the apologetic concern had the effect of obscuring, for example, the deep similarities and differences involved in using scientific models to explain unobservable phenomena (e.g., a black hole) and the religious use of models to accurately describe the transcendent. Nevertheless, in the analytic—and even to some extent in the phenomenological—philosophical tradition, philosophers seeking to rehabilitate religious language drew heavily on cutting-edge philosophy of science. While this was primarily undertaken to undermine the status conferred on scientific inquiry, it had, for our purposes, the beneficial effect of introducing and demonstrating the similarities between the two domains.[5]

It should come as no surprise then that early studies into the possibility of religious language placed a premium on the epistemological problems of onto-theological reference and the standards of verification/falsification. If religious language were to be taken seriously, it had to rise and fall on the same standards set out for the sciences. So the task was twofold: demonstrate that logical positivism was unable to ground actual scientific practice and replace it with a philosophy of language amenable to both the hard sciences and theology—the deposed queen whose throne they had usurped. With respect to grounding actual scientific practice, verification was—even when sympathetically maintained—supplemented with explanations relying on coherence rather than empirical verification.[6] Such studies paved the way for a generous critical realism that takes language "seriously, not literally"[7] and that offers "epistemic access" rather than ontological surety.[8] It is now basically assumed to be the consensus view of language held by scientific and philosophical realists.

These are not, or at least not primarily, the concerns of the present inquiry. The question set before us is not essentially a question of whether religious language can ontically refer since operating from within a Trinitarian framework assumes this possibility from the outset.[9] We will nevertheless want to explore the hows and whys of referring religious language, paying specific attention to the special genius or rhetorical and conceptual effect of religious metaphor. Can a religious metaphor function as a reliable probe into the nature and character of the triune God and the relations holding between this God and human beings? If so, how? From whence do promising linguistic probes arise? Will any metaphor do, or are some more pregnant than others? Of course it will be our ultimate goal to situate the labor pains metaphor within the larger field of theologically pregnant metaphors; demonstrating how and why this is an appropriate move will demand some account of metaphor and its relationship to the language of Christian theology.

In what follows, we will discern four critical elements of religious metaphors that are of particular value to a theologian of the cross, noting along the way the roles they will play in our account. They are (1) lexical adaptation, (2) metaphoric disclosure, (3) irreducible metaphoric meaning, and (4) grounding in Scripture. Lexical adaptation is the process by which semantic fields expand such that our words change in meaning as they are applied to new phenomena. Thus "the labor of God" may have as much to say about birthing labor as it does about the cross of Christ. By metaphoric disclosure, we emphasize the way in which fixing an inappropriate predicate to events or objects in the world first shocks and then helps us discover new things about those events or objects, even setting out paths of potential research. Irreducible metaphoric meaning highlights the ineffability of certain uses of language, demonstrating that good metaphoric use leaves some things mysterious and unrepeatable. If a metaphor is either wholly transparent or wholly opaque, it fails to capture the imagination: it is either flattened and dulled as classical atonement language has become or utterly hermetic. Lastly, we will demonstrate why the Christian atonement theologian must remain in deep conversation with the Bible, as we aim to do theology in keeping with the literary network we receive from the church.

Lexical Adaptation: Gunton, Fields, and Words That Wobble

Couched in the middle of his characterization of the satisfaction/substitution theory of atonement as metaphor, Colin Gunton has this to say:

> The metaphors with which we are concerned in this book have the importance that they do because they help to articulate a central feature of the human condition. It is for that reason that they are finally unfathomable and present to the theologian ever new possibilities for insight and development. For the same reason, no final account can be given of what they mean, certainly not this side of eternity: they are eschatological concepts, giving up their secrets only by anticipation and through the gift of the Spirit.[10]

It is worth highlighting a few assumptions with which Gunton works. First, there is an ineffability to the atonement. We might wonder why it is that certain characterizations of what transpired in the life, death, and resurrection of Jesus present "ever new possibilities for insight and development." Why should they have "no final account"? What is this "central feature of the human condition" to which they bear witness? It is tempting to assume that Gunton is merely gesturing to the inscrutability of the divine in some quasimystical fashion, but this does not appear to be the whole explanation. Rather, the main problem is one of human cognitive limitation. It is an eschatological problem—one that Gunton mentions elsewhere as that ineluctable fact of human living whereby, for now at least, "we know in part" (1 Corinthians 13:9).[11] This is an insurmountable ontological and epistemic gulf between human beings and their creator. The corollary of this observation is that metaphors of the atonement give us some cognitive access not to the ontological reality of the divine but to the *real effects of divine action on us.* As we will see in a moment, it is only insofar as the tangible reality of God's action pushes on our language that we can say with any certainty that atonement-talk offers genuine understanding.

Related to this first observation is the second. Note that it is the metaphors themselves—as opposed to the atonement itself—that "present ever new possibilities for insight and development." How does this work? If it is not the atonement-in-itself that our atonement-talk is about, what real, ontological connection exists between the thing-in-itself and our speech? Gunton's preferred example at this point involves the term "magnetic field."[12] Coined by Michael Faraday,[13] the term "field" had, until the 1840s, never indicated a sphere within which a certain sort of force is exerted at varying degrees. In fact, it did not indicate a sphere of *influence* at all, though it had long been used to identify (metaphorically, of course), say, "fields of inquiry." This is to say that an abstracted notion of the term "field" is well attested, but it appears to be Faraday who introduced the concepts of "force" and "field" to one another. There are two particularly interesting aspects of this union.

In a way, the word field was well suited to technical usage. It was commonplace to think, for example, of a field as a conceptual space. The *Oxford English Dictionary* points us to act 3 of John Dryden's "The Rival Ladies," where Gonsalvo, commenting on the emotional travails of young love, tells Angelina, "Thou hast not field enough in thy young breast / To entertain such storms to struggle in."[14] We could quite easily replace field with "space" or "room" to achieve an equivalent to Dryden's meaning. But we should not overlook the sort of space this is. It is not a physically demarcated area. It is, rather, a place appropriated for a certain kind of activity, a place for emotional travail. In this somewhat abstract usage, one needs only to replace Dryden's "storms" with "magnetic attraction" to get very close to what Faraday will need. Thus, already in the mid-seventeenth century, the English word can carry a part of the full scientific sense with which Faraday would one day imbue it.

What is therefore novel about Faraday's usage is the kind of change the word field must undergo in order to make it a successful metaphor. As it happens, the magnetic force that can be mathematically described around the magnet decreases the farther from the magnet we travel. This is a new concept. Before Faraday's linguistic-theoretical contribution, whatever fell within the province of the field was equally applicable to all portions of the field. Every part of the wheat field is expected to grow wheat. Every portion of Angelina's breast is equally capable (or incapable) of entertaining "such storms." Not so with electromagnetic forces. A magnetic field ebbs and flows according to the distance from the magnet. The meaning of the word itself changes in accordance with its application. The success of this change has been so thorough that it hardly requires explanation, being so pervasive that one certainly need not specialize in field theory to intuit that the strength of "force fields" in science fiction may vary in accordance with their distance from their source. Or, more conventionally, we take it as a matter of fact that the power of a planet's "gravitational field" increases as we come closer to it.

This insight about the way metaphorical application alters words interests Gunton because it demonstrates in a concrete manner how language adapts to the real world. It is worth mentioning that for all our talk of magnetic fields as though they were something we perceive directly, a "magnetic field" is really a linguistic stand-in for a mathematical model based on empirical observations. This is not to say that fields are not ontologically real;[15] it is merely to note that whatever fields may be, we do not have any empirical access to the ontology that undergirds them. So, for example, the standard view among physicists and metaphysicians is that fields have ontic status and an intrinsic nature, but it could be the case that they are merely mathematically specified regions of "categorically ungrounded counterfactuals," meaning that regions are defined only by how they would be observed to act if they were to encounter objects of mass and force.[16]

It might be that physicists, emboldened by the success of mathematical models to describe fields, simply passed over the "epistemological gap." This implies that "a determined metaphysician (or reflective physicist)," however, "will sense many unanswered questions."[17] That is, we use the term as though it picked out some easily appropriated, ontologically obvious thing-in-the-world capable of causation, but this is simply not the case. When iron filaments come under the influence of a magnet, there is a well-attested set of physical descriptions about how they will act, but this puts us no closer to "observing" a magnetic field than it does to observing God. All that is possible is a systematic description of events that appear to conform to law-like behavior.

But, and this is critical, the field metaphor is so useful and successful that the technical term "magnetic field" has been reified. Likewise, we must become aware of the fact that however comfortable we may be with accounts of atonement, they, like magnetic fields, are ultimately metaphorical stand-ins for something that is not—and cannot be—perceived directly. The complete ontological status of atonement, which is to say "whatever happens between God and humanity in and through the career of Jesus Christ," is not the sort of thing to which human beings have unmediated epistemic access. It is within the give and take of metaphorical mediation that our words wobble and stretch as they become adequate to the task of grasping the "causal structures of reality."[18]

With respect to the Christian doctrine of atonement, the unjust murder of a Jewish carpenter for blasphemy and sedition really did something, and our language about that something somehow conforms to it limitedly and yet truly. This is an undoubtedly peculiar idea insofar as it forces us to extrapolate the inner workings of the process. With magnetic fields there is a fairly obvious correlation between the observed events—iron filaments and their consistent, law-like attraction to magnets—and the use of language to set up an epistemic window into their nature. Analogously, how is it that characterizing the death of Jesus by Roman torture as a "victory" conforms to anything that really happened in however limited a fashion? What could possibly explain this bizarre juxtaposition?

Verification, or at least confidence about language's referential purchase, seems to hinge on the success or failure of the metaphor to open us up to discoveries about the world. Following a paper by Richard Boyd,[19] Gunton explains that "the world—if we have found the right metaphor—will enforce, so to speak, changes in the meanings of the words we use."[20] This corresponds to the changes effected on the word field by Faraday's scientific usage. Metaphorical success requires that the cosmos "push back" on our linguistic novelties in such a way that our words begin to teach us new things about that cosmos.[21] But this requires us to rethink what it is that is happening when, to put it bluntly, metaphors are coined. Richard Boyd writes, "We introduce terminology to refer to presumed kinds of natural phenomena long before our study of them has progressed to the point where we can specify for them the sort of defining conditions that the positivist's account of language would require. The introduction of theoretical terms does require, however, some tentative or preliminary indication of the properties of the presumed kinds in question."[22] The introduction of metaphors in science and, as Boyd argues, in language generally, operates intuitively. It happens pretheoretically, and, therefore, it is a feature of the "causal structures of reality" that they "will enforce, so to speak, changes in the meanings of the words we use." The operant image—one reinforced by, among others, Kuhn—is of sudden insight that produces linguistic novelty and that is later confirmed by observation and subsequent discovery. It is, according to this theory, a reality of the cosmos that the space—the field—of magnetic attraction designates a real place in which real forces are exerted with real, varying degrees. Fields, as it were, are more than we thought. Faraday's linguistic novelty created conceptual space for the universe to teach us a thing or two.

With respect to the atonement, Gunton draws our attention to classical concepts like sacrifice and victory. Of course no standard definition of victory or sacrifice could be instantiated in the grisly murder of an innocent itinerant healer/exorcist, but there, we might say, is the rub. If we want to understand *real* victory, *real* sacrifice, we must consider the career of Jesus of Nazareth. The universe has a few more things to teach, and, with the aid of these new linguistic probes, we are given the conceptual room to work out an account of how strange descriptors can make sense of and thus transform our notions about what sacrifice and victory are. The very story of Jesus will assert itself against our language and alter it appropriately.

Our account of atonement metaphors must therefore be a two-way street. Not only do the inappropriate predicates teach us about Jesus' career, but Jesus' career should significantly alter the semantic associations we hold with respect to the inappropriate predicate. Religious metaphor, whatever else it may be, is not a static descriptor of divine reality. Atonement metaphors ought to instruct us in surprising, even shocking, ways.[23]

Reading the Fourth Gospel's crucifixion account as a particular kind of birth scene therefore functions as the pretheoretical moment of insight that is minted in language. This crucifixion is different from the others because it is the once-and-for-all moment of spiritual birth. This instance of Roman torture is different from the others because it, unlike the others, is the Second Person of the Trinity's pangs in childbirth. In this moment of insight, everything is thrown into flux: crucifixion, labor, birth, and God. The moment of insight opens up the opportunity for a conceptual reconfiguration that will, if true, "stick" linguistically. It will "catch on" because subsequent reflection on initial pretheoretical insight will confirm that these two conceptual domains have greater interaction than we otherwise might have suspected.

The aim of the present study, then, will be to understand what we learn about God and crucifixion when we begin to understand it as birthing labor. There will be systematic fallout: fresh notions of atonement will lead to rereckonings of other theological domains. And the street will be two-way: introducing the notion of crucifixion and atonement to maternal labor will suggest a rereckoning of what it is to give birth. The travail metaphor, having linguistically and conceptually encountered the cross, pushes against and ultimately transforms our notion of maternal labor. Perhaps a sustained treatment of the metaphor as it appears throughout the Scriptures will press our theological conception of childbirth and even womanhood in surprising—and hopefully edifying—directions.

Metaphoric Disclosure: Models in Scientific and Religious Inquiry

Leading the charge in the twentieth century's quasi-apologetic vindication of religious language was the Anglican philosopher/theologian Ian Ramsey. Ramsey's work largely involved drawing out the significance of the role of metaphorical models in both scientific and religious language, demonstrating their use as both analogical and disclosing.[24] Placing emphasis on the centrality of models to the actual work of science does the heavy lifting, allowing Ramsey to develop an account of theological language that conforms (broadly) to reigning scientific paradigms, highlighting the justificatory roles of empirical fit, adequacy, coherence, and authentic belief.[25] But it is his development of the role of models in science and religion that are of particular interest to the theologian of the atonement. As Soskice explains it, "A good model suggests possibilities."[26] To take a favored example, scientists will sometimes compare light—when viewed as particles—to billiards. So the interaction of particles is conceived of as billiard balls colliding and separating. Analogically, there are some properties that light-as-particles and billiard balls share, namely, the aforementioned propensity to bounce off each other. But there are many ways in which billiard balls and light are certainly different. For example, light-as-particles does not have little numbers printed on each particle; billiard balls do. Such traits are deemed conceptually fruitless. There is no need to consider that particular aspect of a billiard ball as a way to understand light better. There may, however, be some traits that colliding spheres possess that may or may not be of value when thinking about light. These are sometimes called "neutral analogies," because they suggest avenues for further research. In the present case, something like vector or velocity may be of interest when thinking about light. The conceptual model, introduced by the metaphor, opens up opportunities for novel and unexpected research possibilities.[27] So it is that a scientific model is really just a metaphor that has been systematized.[28] The lure of metaphors and models for the theologian is clear: a metaphor for the relationship between human beings and God might be systematized in ways that offer constructive theological probes into that relationship. Just as billiard balls might suggest avenues of research, so might a metaphor for God—such as "God is our father"—be systematized and integrated into revelation and experience so that we might credibly account for who God is and what God's "fatherliness" actually looks like in the world.

Consider this example, "Our love is a battlefield." How does this metaphor work? It could be that the metaphorical battlefield operates as an implicit model or lens through which we "view" our love. By appropriating certain features of the model analogically (e.g., hotly contested positions, two opposing forces, and so forth), the metaphor discloses heretofore unnoticed features of the world of our love.[29] What matters here is what we normally associate with battlefields and whether these commonplace assumptions about what battlefields are like apply analogically to the subject of the metaphorical statement. What the battlefield model has not yet done, however, is disclose new possible ways of learning about our love. For this, it might be helpful to turn briefly to the main topic of our inquiry: atonement.

Now consider this statement, "Jesus' death is the labor of God." On an analogical account the meaning of this statement and the truth-conditionals against which its accuracy is adjudicated arise from our conceptions about the travails of childbirth. The metaphor invites us

into the extended image or model of birth. Within this model, we identify the salient, analogous features, like pain and spilling blood, noting that both are present at Jesus' execution.[30] We discard the obvious
irregularities, such as the fact that Jesus does not possess reproduc-
tive organs like a uterus, as unimportant for the analogy. Lastly, we
identify those elements that are suggestive for further research. In this
case, we note that, for example, successful labor results in the birth of
a healthy child. Ostensibly, these "neutral" elements—those with an
analogical nature about which we remain agnostic—point us toward
imaginative and potentially illuminating similarities. Perhaps it is the
case that Jesus' death on the cross could be understood as the way
in which God labored with and then gave birth to spiritual children
(John 3:3-7). If this is indeed the case, then a number of theological
implications immediately present themselves. Who are God's spiritual children, and what is their relationship to Jesus' execution? What
might a "healthy spiritual child" look like? What are the implications
for the God-born of being birthed into God's family? These are just
a few other neutral analogies suggested by the labor metaphor as a
model for understanding Jesus' death.

Above, we noted that a successful metaphor adapts to the "causal
structures of reality." In the case of metaphoric disclosure, we may
make some concrete suggestions as to how this happens. The novel feature of Faraday's magnetic field, as we saw, was the varying presence
of force in different regions of the field. In terms of metaphoric disclosure, we can make the following analysis. Insofar as a wheat field is a
demarcated area set apart for a particular activity, the "field model" has
two positive analogies to what we empirically observe around a magnet. This leads to a further question. Do magnetic forces act equally
in various locations within the region of the field? Of course they do
not. The model discloses to us dissimilarities between the inappropriate predicate and the subject, either demanding that the metaphor be
discarded or pressing the predicate to adapt semantically. But notice
that it is sustained consideration of the model and the world of the
model that clarifies these metaphoric relations. This analysis gives us
a bit more insight into how we sort positive and negative analogies
cognitively. The model, if it is to disclose anything, must suppress certain elements of the subject and/or predicate's semantic field. With
long use and lexical adaptation, it should be no surprise, then, that the

Christian metaphorical use of "sacrifice" for Jesus' death on the cross develops a semantic field all its own, one in which "spotless lambs" and "scapegoats" may not necessarily be found near the center.

Note also that sustained reflection on this metaphor has theological implications that may run far and wide, just as reflecting deeply on, say, the battlefield of love may have serious implications for one's decision to continue a relationship. Likewise, however viewing the cross as labor might expand or alter atonement theology, it will also likely invite revision or at least reconsideration of other doctrinal commitments. Doing theology with metaphors requires both tacit admission that doctrines are not hermetically sealed off from each other and some commitment to seeing through the conceptual implications of this or that belief.

With respect to divine travail, there is a further question that must be addressed. If travail is to be a suitable model for atonement, we might expect to have to develop a clear set of associations, each of which can be identified as a positive, negative, or neutral analogy to the career of Jesus. It may be the case, however, and this is what I will argue below, that our commonsense conceptions of labor, birth, and semantically related lexemes are not by themselves enough to ground a robust constructive theology of atonement. Instead, because our notions of labor, birth, and, as we will see, violence, sin, and gender— among other elements—need to change as they are disclosed in the light of the cross and Scripture, the rigor with which we think in terms of analogy will be softened. Metaphorical meanings are not so clearly delineated. In fact, it is the nature of metaphor to be slippery in just this way. A satisfactory account of metaphor in religious language must be able to address the special and irreducible nature of metaphorical meaning.

Metaphoric Meaning: That Which Cannot Be Communicated in Any Other Way

Surely one of the more dispiriting aspects of the present moment in atonement theology is its dearth of poetry. "Poetry" not in the sense of meter and verse but in the aesthetic sense, the raw emotive grip that must accompany any faithful transmission of the gospel of a crucified God. Here, Christianity's greatest success is also its downfall, such that baseball players and pop stars alike wear a cross—a cross!—about their necks as jewelry. The language of the cross as, for example, a sacrifice or a substitution slides in and out of ears without a second thought because there is nothing left of these images that remains undisclosed, mysterious, or unsaid. In their common use, these images leave nothing to the imagination at all, functioning as little more than ciphers for a clean exchange between God—who is said to be ineffable and therefore, it would seem, beyond such an economy—and human beings. The cross now fits neatly on a chain because, whatever else its wearers might think about it, it is not dangerous; it is not dangerous partly because it makes perfect, transparent sense. As we will now see, however, this is just another way of saying that "sacrifice" has stopped being a metaphor at all. It is just common discourse and therefore inadequate to the subject about which it purports to speak. Metaphorical language is appropriate to God precisely because it holds something back.

At the heart of her *Metaphor and Religious Language*, Janet Martin Soskice carves out an account of metaphorical language that preserves the uniqueness, the creativity, the novelty, and the irreducible meaning of metaphorical statements. Following an example drawn from Woolf's *To the Lighthouse*, she writes:

> The metaphor and its meaning (it is artificial to separate them) are the unique product of the whole and the excellence of a metaphor such as this one is not that it is a new description of a previously discerned human condition but that this subject, this particular mental state, is accessible only through the metaphor. What is identified and described is identified and described uniquely by this metaphor. It is in this way that a metaphor is genuinely creative and says something that can be said adequately in no other way, not as an ornament to what we already know but as an embodiment of a new insight.[31]

A living, vital metaphor communicates something new, and it does so in a unique and irreplaceable way. In this particular case, Woolf's metaphor for terrible grief requires the collision of two sets of semantic domains: the set associated with grief and the set issued by her description of what appears to be a well in which a single drop of water—a tear—falls down the shaft and is swallowed up into the pool at the bottom. Woolf's control of the narrative and her particular weaving of this literary vehicle for the metaphor infuse the description with a quality that cannot be reduced to more mundane language. To paraphrase the metaphor as something like "a lonesome sadness" just does not adequately describe what Woolf has depicted in the extended metaphor.

Such an example is attractive because it resists mere analogical interpretation. That is, no amount of "viewing grief" from the lens of a teardrop falling down a well will provide the right set of positive, negative, and neutral analogies needed to understand this grief. This aesthetic quality of the metaphor's communication provides an artistic complement to the analytical aspects of the way metaphors convey meaning. The models that images suggest possess value, but not exhaustively so. These words and their semantic ranges juxtaposed just so, located in just this sort of literary context, and rolling off the tongue in just this way produce a metaphorical effect, one identified wholly and completely with *this* instance of *this* particular grief. In short, the metaphor's meaning is irreducible.

It may be best to supplement an analytical account of metaphor with a phenomenological account. And while we may ultimately have qualms about fully embracing Paul Ricoeur's theory of split reference, it will be helpful to retain at least its spirit. Consider the well-known black-and-white image that can be seen either as a vase or as two faces looking at one another.[32] The image demonstrates pictorially the sort of cognitive process Ricoeur believes to be at work in the apprehension of a metaphor. We view the image one way or the other, and we do so *in toto*. What happens visually in this case happens linguistically and semantically in metaphorical utterance. And lest we too hastily discard the metaphor of perception to get at the thing-in-itself, we should remember that Aristotle is Ricoeur's departure point for the theory of metaphor.[33] Among other things Ricoeur gleans from the philosopher, Ricoeur supposes that successful metaphors are an example of perceiving a single genus that undergirds two seemingly disparate semantic fields.[34] Of course this insight too relies on a metaphor—distance, that is, farness and nearness—but it designates for us what it is, exactly, to which a metaphor refers. The metaphor picks out by linguistic genesis the overlap between two semantic fields that do not and cannot literally obtain. The result is primarily a phenomenological insight wherein two literally unrelated classes are perceived as identical. Ricoeur, borrowing from the literary theory of his own context, calls this "imagistic" or "figurative style." His language indicates that he means by this much the same thing that Soskice deems the "vehicle," that unique authorial shaping that infuses a metaphor with the irreplaceable and irreducible nature of its meaning.[35]

Wading a bit further into the phenomenological stream, what happens at the moment of metaphor is pretheoretical and, given the value of the visual metaphor, aesthetic. Linguistic novelty creates juxtapositions that force us to view the subject in just this way, as it were, as two faces and not a vase. The inappropriate predicate conjures a mapping of the subject that, because it is not literally possible, requires what Ricoeur, borrowing from Kant, calls "productive imagination." A nonimagistic but iconic world opens up, one that can "point towards original resemblances, whether of quality, structure or locality, of situation, or, finally, of feeling."[36] Language forges a common conceptual genus, a shared substrate between two previously unrelated semantic fields. So it is that grief is "seen as" a tear falling down a well. We are pressed into using a visual metaphor here; perhaps what we are describing is irreducibly metaphorical.

It is at this point worth wondering if metaphorical language that does not hold something back, that is not in some way irreducible, is truly metaphor at all. Fundamentally, we are asking if it is the case that some language that began as metaphor has degenerated into cipher or something else, perhaps allegory.[37] For example, I might say, "That guy is a snake," and be perfectly happy to have "a snake" replaced with "sneaky" or "a liar." This is not a minor point; we are not quibbling over labels because it might be the case that a great deal of our language about the atonement has become inert precisely because it has become cipher or allegorical. The problem is not that there is something special about metaphors that make them somehow linguistically superior to other types of discourse. Rather, the problem is that religious language attempts to gain purchase on an ineffable God. Where the metaphor has—due either to overuse or to overanalysis or both—become transparent in meaning, it can no longer truly speak of a categorically transcendent God. Where once it probed and revealed and disclosed and then ceased to speak when it reached places thoughts dare not tread, it at some point reaches beyond its ken and, to borrow the language of continental philosophy, attempts to overcome God in a totalizing fashion.

This is, of course, why a retrieval of the labor pain metaphor is essential at the present moment; classical formulations have been mapped onto theory so entirely that they reduce the infinite to that which can be spoken by the finite. Rather than repeating the language of sacrifice or victory or ransom or influence, pastoral theology would do better to complicate it, bedim it, point out its inconsistencies, and recapture its mysteries. The labor metaphor provides superior epistemic access to the divine in part because the shocking power of its juxtaposition has not yet been rigorously and exhaustively conceptually mapped. The bizarre discordances between the image of a birthing mother and a blasphemer's crucifixion have not been ironed and smoothed and then erased. Not to put too fine a point on it, well-meaning theologians have not yet demystified those discordances with the cold light of systematizing reason. All of this should be taken as a caution. Our constructive work has limits we would do well to respect. The labor of God is not a scientific theory. It is not a conceptual box into which God neatly fits. It is rather a faithful means of theological reflection. And that should be enough.

It remains to be shown, however, why it is that labor pain is a "faithful means" of reflection on the cross. For that matter, it is worth explaining why any particular linguistic probe into the divine generally and atonement specifically can say anything true at all. We will now entertain this final concern.

Appropriate for Christian Theology: Religious Metaphors and the Scriptures

In one essay, Ricoeur traces the use of linguistic philosophy in the work of some philosophers of science who apply the idea of metaphor to scientific models. Then, seeing how they used and adapted hermeneutics to describe how scientific models operate and develop, Ricoeur sees fit to borrow back these newer insights. He recaps:

> [W]hat on the poetic side corresponds exactly to the model is not precisely what we have called the "metaphorical statement," that is, a short bit of discourse reduced most often to a sentence. Rather, as the model consists in a complex network of statements, its exact analogue would be the extended metaphor—tale, allegory. What Toulmin calls the "systematic deployability"

of the model finds its equivalent in a metaphoric network and not in an isolated metaphor.[38]

The depth and richness of Ricoeur's insights here require a few explanatory remarks: by "model," Ricoeur refers to a scientific model such as field theory. The "poetic side" refers to a particular type of discourse that Ricoeur has borrowed from Aristotle. The poetical is any mode of discourse—fiction, tale, poem, allegory, myth—concerned with "an essential representation of human actions."[39] That is, it is impossible accurately to describe human action in a scientific sense. There is simply too much going on—desires, perceptions, emotions, reasons—to get a fully scientific explanation of what humans do and experience. It is therefore the realm of poetics to tell the truth about these sorts of issues in a way that scientific description cannot. Common methods for accomplishing this task include plot, characters, diction, metaphor, and so on.

In this way we see how it is possible to appropriate a tool of scientific inquiry—the model—to help explain how it is that an extended work of the poetical can in fact truly map out what is happening in the world. Recalling our discussion of magnetic fields, what makes the field metaphor effective and deployable is not merely the metaphorical alteration of the word "field" by itself. Field theory must be integrated into a larger network of metaphors if it is to be of any use. The result is something like a set of interrelated metaphorical nodes, each describing a scientific domain, and each in a relationship of mutual interpretation with the other nodes. So the field model is embedded within a larger set of models like vector, tension, force, and boundary.[40] The good scientific theory systematically describes and relates these regions of metaphorical models such that, for example, alterations in the force and vector of iron filings may be described as they interact with the magnetic field. The theory organizes and explains the relationships between as many of the models as possible. The greater the organizational and explanatory success, the stronger the theory. Metaphors within, say, a poem, take the form of a network as well. And an interpretation of the poem, like a scientific theory, organizes and explains how individual metaphors relate to one another. Here, again, we turn to Ricoeur:

Metaphoricity is a trait not only of [individual metaphors] but of [the entire plot] itself; and, as in the case of models, this metaphoricity consists in describing a less known domain—human reality—in the light of relationships within a fictitious but better known domain—the tragic tale—utilizing all the strengths of "systematic deployability" contained in that tale. . . . What Aristotle himself emphasized . . . is that poetry is closer to essence than is history, which is preoccupied with the accidental. Tragedy teaches us to "see" human life "as" that which the [the entire plot] displays.[41]

A tragic tale, or really any extended work of creative organization, has this essential metaphoricity: by developing a network of metaphors, the tale creates a vision of human existence that replaces, or perhaps supersedes, the mere stringing together of accidents. By viewing human life through the lens of tragedy, what might otherwise appear to be random and chaotic is understood to be tragic instead. Moreover, individual metaphors gain and sustain their currency only when embedded within this larger metaphoric network. Apart from a narrative, then, calling Jesus a sacrifice is just a shade more than calling Jesus nothing at all. That is, at the level of the sentence, the inappropriate predicate—in this case, "sacrifice"—is nearly devoid of content. When supplied with a rich context like, say, the cultic system developed in the Pentateuch and relativized in the prophets, calling Jesus a sacrifice begins to take on meaning. Going further, if the sacrificial Jesus is *embedded* into this larger story as a part of its continuance or even its culmination, then what was once merely or only contextual becomes transformative and so sets the stage for the development of a theory. Moreover, the notion of atonement itself, that is, the "at-oneing" of God and humanity, only makes sense within a larger—indeed cosmic—narrative. Just as the individual metaphor fits into a larger set of nodes and thereby alters the entire web with its introduction, so does atonement itself take its meaning from a larger theological context and then subsequently send out doctrinal ripples on its insertion. In short, one's doctrine of God both sets the stage for a theology of atonement and is then impacted as atonement conceptually settles into the larger theological tapestry. Returning for a moment to scientific models, this is analogous to the process by which the individual metaphorical model "magnetic field" gets taken up into a mathematical relationship with other descriptive metaphors such as "vector" and "force" to create a scientific theory.

Put this way, the Christian theologian can see why it is that the Christian canon provides the literary network within which an individual atonement metaphor may be taken up in a model featuring mutually interpreting nodes. First, both Old and New Testament Scriptures assume a universe in which the divine and the human interact. This corresponds to what Ricoeur thinks of as the poetical. Whereas historical investigation cannot proceed unless it categorically excludes the possibility of divine action, the Scriptures assume the opposite to be the case. In the world of the Bible, it makes sense that historical events may be truly interpreted as mediating divine and human relationships. Moreover, by placing the New Testament writings subsequent to Israel's Scriptures, the ordering of the canon itself suggests that the Gospels continue the story told by the law, the writings, and the prophets. However Jesus' career is described, it is preceded by Israel's rise and fall. Ignoring this context is like performing only the play's last act: there will be no catharsis because there has been no conflict.

Second, the New Testament writers assume continuity between the story of Israel and the life, death, and resurrection of Jesus the Nazarene. In fact, there is a sense in which the Hebrew Scriptures must ratify Christian proclamation and Christian Scriptures as truly in keeping with the nature, character, and story of the God of Israel. When the church was in its infancy, the Old Testament was not a negotiable element in theological reflection; it was the basis of theological reflection. If Jesus was to be known as the Jewish messiah, then Jesus had to be understood within the context of Jewish reflection on the Jewish messiah. As Robert Jenson puts it, "Israel's Scripture accepted—or did not accept—the church."[42]

Put another way, the stories, themes, and theology of the New Testament are explicitly contextualized by an appeal to Israel's Scriptures. So it is that the first chapter of Hebrews claims that the words of David in Psalm 45:6-7 are addressed to the Son of God (Hebrews 1:8-9). Luke 24:25-27 also makes this kind of thinking explicit when Jesus converses with Cleopas and his companion on the road to Emmaus. To speak of David witnessing or prophesying about Christ or to suggest that Jesus could point to "the things concerning himself" (τὰ περὶ ἑαυτοῦ) in Moses and the Prophets presupposes a world in which the meaning of the Messiah's career is bound to and located in Israel's Scriptures. As we attempt atonement theology in our context, we are wise to continue this trajectory. By standing within a preexisting tradition of appealing to the Scriptures, we are able to do theology in the same way that the author of Hebrews does theology. Hebrews not only assumes the aforementioned narratival continuity with Israel's Scriptures; it likewise contextualizes *atonement language* within Israel's story. So, for example, Hebrews 9:11-14 explains the supremacy of Jesus' priesthood in terms of a sacrifice of "his own blood." The logic of the letter insists that Jesus' ability to mediate between human beings and God is predicated on his continuity with and superiority to the traditional mediators—the priests—of the Old Testament. If we are to develop a fresh model of atonement, we too may seek to be in keeping with the *lexis* and *muthos* of the Scriptures. Theology now bears an analogical relationship to the theology of the authors of the New Testament: what has come before and been ratified by the Spirit—in our case, the Christian canon, and, in the case of the first Christians, Israel's Scriptures—provides the textual context from which metaphorical theology springs.

All of this is to say that metaphors embedded in the Scriptures hold a special pride of place in Christian atonement theology. By presupposing the literary network that developed around God and God's life with Israel and then the whole world, the salient metaphors derived from the Old and New Testaments properly embed the life, death, and resurrection of Israel's Messiah within its religious *muthos*. Moreover, in the previous section we noted the importance of the fact that metaphors—while possessing the conceptual currency to suggest models through which we investigate the atonement—must nevertheless resist the reducible systematization of a scientific theory in order to retain something of the ineffability appropriate to their divine subject. If this is in fact so, it will be the literary network that emerges from the canon that infuses a particular metaphor—in our case travail—with that irreducible, irreplaceable quality. It will be one of our ultimate aims to argue not only that a mother's labor in birth affords us a model from which we can develop constructive theological probes but that the rich literary tapestry of the Scriptures imbues it with a unique and irreducible metaphorical meaning.

The Way Forward

Our inquiry into the philosophy of religious language—specifically metaphor—offers four major takeaways. First, we have seen that metaphor forces unexpected changes in a word or words' semantic field(s). These changes correspond to the pressing of the real world onto the language we use to describe it. In the present case, this will force us to consider how seeing the violence of the cross as maternal labor alters the way we think about maternity and labor just as it expands the way we think about Jesus' death and atonement. We then saw that metaphors in religious language will work much as they do in scientific inquiry. Specifically, good religious metaphors will invite further inquiry and discovery, opening up dark theological corners to linguistic light. We saw thirdly that all good metaphors must remain in some ways opaque. The goal is not, as the logical positivists thought, to reduce all language to symbolic logic. It is instead to allow some things to be known only in a particular way as the fallout from the clash between two semantic fields. Lastly, we argued for the Christian canon as the primary ground for religious language that relates to the atonement. To put it crudely, we receive in the Scriptures the "story so far," the literary network that has been given to the church. Only by remaining deeply conversant with this network of metaphors are we able to make sense of how a Roman cross could be anything other than a Roman cross, let alone the labor of God to birth spiritual children into the world.

The atonement language found in the Scriptures has pushed atonement theology in particular directions, such that "violence" and "sin" are tightly bound to the semantic field conjured by the word "atonement." But what happens when we inject the fresh insights of a new and different metaphorical model to aging theological controversies? What might we learn of violence and sin when we take seriously the notion that the cross is the labor of God to give birth to spiritual children? How might our notions of gender wobble and stretch when we commit to the notion that Jesus of Nazareth died in childbirth? Or what might it say of Christian identity and ethics if we are God-born in some real, ontological sense? How are we to think of the gift of the Spirit as processing through the Word's labor? What does it mean for the Word's participation in first creation and the election of Israel if labor is a part of God's generative acts?

We have so far seen that metaphorical models can open up paths to religious discovery. Metaphor resists thoroughgoing systematization, but it does offer analogies that can push language to change as we encounter new theological landscapes. The reality of what has transpired between God and humanity is too great to be captured in any one metaphor or image, but, as we will now see, (re)claiming travail as an atonement metaphor gives us a way forward in a number of contemporary debates because it reframes those debates in critically important ways. In conversation with the Scriptures, Christian theology, and philosophy, the labor of God at the cross may help us better grasp the roles of violence, sin, the procession of the Spirit, and creative acts in the economy of God.

3

CONVERTING THE CROSS
How Torture Becomes Childbirth

Cynthia Crysdale begins her theology of suffering by relating her experience of childbirth. She testifies:

> In all my life so far I have never been as physically vulnerable nor as close to the pulse of death and life as I was that night. I had never experienced pain so directly and so intensely. The next morning I told my husband, "Last night was the most horrible night of my life." Then I added, "Last night was the most wonderful night of my life." For days and weeks I pondered over this simultaneity of joy and suffering. For the first time I began to grasp the way in which death might not be as fearful as I had imagined. I could see, as I never had before, that death might be intensely painful and yet transformative. I pondered the notion that death and resurrection might just happen at the same time. One single insight gradually emerged: resurrection joy does not come *after* crucifixion pain, it is the same thing![1]

For Crysdale, the joy of creation is bound up with, and perhaps even generated by, its humbling, excruciating cost. Perhaps she echoes the words of Jesus in John 16:21: "When a woman is in labor, she has pain, because her hour has come. But when her child is born, she no longer remembers the anguish because of the joy of having brought a human being into the world." If so, her experience challenges the words of the Gospel in two ways. First, Crysdale most assuredly "remembers the anguish" of her experience.[2] Second, and more importantly, Crysdale retrospectively merges the experiences of joy and suffering. Linearly, it would be hard to deny that labor brought extraordinary pain that was succeeded by the immeasurable joy of receiving her newborn. In a real way, however, the suffering, the damage her body endures, is constitutive of the joy of new birth. The child does not "make the pain or the stretch marks worth it" as that formulation misses her insight. What Crysdale seems to be saying is that part of the joy of "bringing a human being into the world" is the extraordinary pain and bodily harm by which it comes. This should seem jarring to us from a theological perspective because Crysdale has just argued not only that suffering can sometimes be a good—for we suppose that the Christian tradition could hardly dispute that notion—but that it is a necessary component of some kinds of good—one of which, if the cross is the labor of God, is atonement. Pain and injury to a woman's body in childbirth are both essential to childbirth and, mysteriously, constitutive of the joy it engenders. In the face of much current atonement theology, then, Crysdale asserts that, yes, the violence of the cross is quite necessary, that God could not have "resurrection joy" without "crucifixion pain" because the two are, in some strange way, "the same thing."

Thinking atonement in labor terms will therefore revitalize worn out, tired debates about violence and atonement, reconfiguring them with new possibility. Rather than categorically rejecting any association between God and violence, the labor metaphor juxtaposes a violent death on a cross with a harmful, but generative and sacral, birth scene, bringing them together without rearranging our portrait of the Christian God into a bloodthirsty tyrant or an abusive parent. It helps us make sense of violent necessity as something creative and deeply profound. Jesus is neither murdered child nor passive victim; instead, Jesus is the divine mother who willingly and capably bears the cost of spiritual birth. The theological implications range far and wide. Because the sufferings of the cross are birthing travails, we can interpret them as necessary to God's project of atonement and simultaneously nonviolent in ways that should assuage some traditional critiques of, for example, penal substitutionary atonement. Because the suffering is necessary but nonviolent, there are ramifications for a Christian doctrine of God—especially with respect to divine impassibility—as well as a doctrine of creation. In short, recovering labor affords atonement theology a chance to again speak new things. The cross' call can once again shock us with news of a God who is with and for human-ity in extremis and in the most radically peaceful way, for this God endures death and transforms it into the pain that accompanies new life. This God can take an instrument of horrific pain, shame, humil-iation, and death and change it utterly, converting it into the ultimate symbol of birth.

The Necessity of Violence for Atonement

It is not uncommon for academic theology to excoriate any notion that the violence of the cross is either necessary or good. We may trace the contemporary trend to the 1977 publication of the English transla-tion of René Girard's *Violence and the Sacred*.[3] Noting the pervasion of sacrifice in early human cultures, Girard makes an anthropologi-cal argument for the necessity of scapegoating in human civilization. Typically, sacrifice is required when major taboos have been violated and/or to mark the sacred nature of certain individuals in the society (such as kings, who, once immolated, are said to be gods). Its logic must be mysterious, and, by galvanizing a community to focus its unspoken tensions on the scapegoat, it allows society as a whole to continue to function by executing a small minority at various intervals. Whatever we make of the historicity of this telling, as an anthropological critique of the logic of sacrifice it has been powerfully influential, and, given the New Testament's proclivity to associate Jesus' death with the sac-rificial cult, it has opened the door to a number of theological critiques of the role of the cross in atonement.

Interestingly, Girard himself supposes that the Scriptures tell the story in which sacrifice itself is exposed as fraudulent, that Jesus' death—as it was put recently—"saves us from [the practice of] sac-rifice."[4] On this account, scapegoating is "the prototypical 'good bad thing' in human culture, a calibrated dose of unjust violence that wards off wider, unrestrained violence." It is "one of the deepest structures of human sin, built into our religion and our politics" and is "demonic because it is endlessly flexible in its choice of prey and because it can truly deliver the good that it advertises." Most importantly, it is "most effective where it is most invisible."[5] The Scriptures offer up a protest, as the marginalized scapegoats are given a voice and name themselves victims rather than "criminals or gods." These are the anonymous voices of psalmists, the complaints of Job, and, ultimately, the cries of

Jesus of Nazareth, whose words on the cross, "Father, forgive them; for they do not know what they are doing" (Luke 23:34 NRSV), take on a kind of prophetic quality when read from a Girardian perspective. Jesus is being scapegoated, but only he knows it. Subsequent reflection on his life and the story of the Scriptures as a whole exposes what sacrifice is and how it truly and effectively restrains mass violence by releasing that violence in a measured dose, destroying the lives of a few that the many might live in peace. We are encouraged to sense something of the church fathers' fascination with the idea of a divine trap: that Satan and his minions are tricked into executing Jesus. Believing that disposing of Jesus (as they have every other scapegoat) will result in the continuance of their demonic power, they unwittingly sow the seeds of their own destruction. As Girard puts it, "The crucifixion of Jesus is a victim mechanism like the others; it is set in motion and develops like the others. Yet its outcome is different from all the others."[6] The resurrection sets off a reversal of the contagion of violence wherever the word of the cross is proclaimed.

Of course such a reading of the cross must account for the fact that Christianity has not actually been a religion that has always and everywhere exposed sacrificial mechanisms and eschewed violence. For Girard's part, his conviction is that this has been due to the loss of the duping of the devil—who is himself but a cipher for the cycles of violence plaguing human communities—in Western theology. If only we had eyes to see and ears to hear, it seems, the true message of the Scriptures—their unmasking and castration of the victim mechanism in human societies—would be heralded as they were always meant to have been.

What Is "Violence"?

Girard's work has not necessarily spawned all of the various critiques of satisfaction or penal substitution theories of atonement, but it does share with them assumptions about the nature of sacrificial violence: that such violence is evil, that it has no place being associated with God, and that it must in every form be expunged and never, ever predicated of God. This raises the obvious question: What is sacrificial violence? And, concordantly, exactly what kind of relationship does God have with violence? In what follows I argue that knowing the cross as divine labor offers a new way of thinking through that question. In the labor of the cross, God does not perpetrate or merely endure violence but instead transforms it into a generative act. To make this case, we must first establish the nature of violence. If what we are talking about is simply harm or injury suffered by one party on behalf of another, then we would have a hard time suggesting that Jesus of Nazareth was not engaged in "sacrificial violence" when he was ruining the businesses of the temple merchants: a few merchants are whipped and a few tables overthrown in order to put many own-ers of many such tables on notice.

In the case of Jesus' cleansing of the temple, violence appears to be not the lash alone but the fear of the lash as well. Coercion itself looks to be a form of violence. The conflation of "violence" and "coercion" in contemporary ethical discourse issues from a rights-based notion of human autonomy and human integrity. Originally formalized by phi-losopher Robert Nozick,[7] coercion is understood to be any situation in which Agent A undertakes action X because Agent B has threatened A with action Y if A fails to do X. Because A judges it better to do X than suffer Y, A does X. Notice that the argument defines coercion in terms of individual autonomy and the fear of harm induced by a threat, which, it should be added, may be either implicit or explicit. Thus, our notion of violence too is implicated: a psychological state of fear or anxiety results in external actions. Harm—at least the psychological sort—is constitutive, though not exhaustively so, of coercion. And it is intuitively tempting to characterize the harm initiated by coercion as "violent."

Moreover, paradigmatic rational agents are needed to make sense of the psychological aspect of the act. Coercion depends on human agents performing a hedonic calculus in order to make a determination about particular goods and the best ways to achieve them. Coercion is itself simply the introduction of the threat of harm in order to push the outcome of said deliberation in a direction more favorable to B than A. Given the extraordinary influence of this kind of definition, we can see why it is that "violence" and "coercion" are bound up with one another in our usage. The effect has been so thorough that advocates of concep-tual nonviolence feel compelled to lament that "we have no term that carries the specific meaning of coercion used positively."[8]

If coercion and violence are inextricably bound up, then we cannot deny that Jesus of Nazareth—to say nothing of the God who commands Israel to commit the Canaanites to *hērem* (i.e., "ritual destruction")—does engage in violent behavior. In order to say otherwise, we must develop an account of acts of coercion, force, and harm that are indeed coercive, forceful, and harmful but, nevertheless, "nonviolent." J. Denny Weaver suggests that such an act deploys a "force or social coercion that respects bodily integrity."[9] Therefore, separating coercion, force, and harm from "violence" depends on preserving a telos both for the one(s) coerced and for the act in question. Unpacking Weaver's "bodily integrity" will help draw this out.

Since nonviolent coercion might harm, for example, institutions, we may rightly surmise that "body" is not shorthand for "individual, autonomous, rational agent," nor is "integrity" something along the lines of "maintaining one's physical, compositional, and psychological status quo." To borrow from the tradition of nonviolence advocated perhaps most famously by Walter Wink, the paradigmatic nonviolent response to hostile powers, that is, Jesus', "aims at converting the opponent."[10] Of course the term "convert" is fraught, so we need to update the argot, such that Jesus "demonstrated an assertive and confrontational nonviolence that provides an opponent with an opportunity for transformation."[11] Armed with this further explanation of how Jesus could be coercive in a godly way, we may excise "coercion" from the discourse of violence entirely; it may not have anything to do with violence at all. Violence properly defined, that is, understood in light of Christian ends, is something like harm that normally hinders or is intended to hinder Godward transformation. One's autonomy or one's rational evaluation of goods—these have little to do with "bodily integrity." Bodily integrity is something more like the ability of an individual or a community to mirror its eschatological self. Where this is hindered, violence; where it is respected, nonviolence. Abstracted from a theological context, "bodily integrity" self-deconstructs. If there is no ultimate end, no communion with the divine, no *imago Dei* to recover, then, and this is critical, *violence is all in all.* Absenting the theological telos renders every interaction necessarily coercive. The question is not whether coercion is present; the question is only whether it succeeds. And now, primed with a teleological account of the nature of violence, we turn to the task of reckoning God's relationship to the violence of crucifixion.

Crucifixion and Childbirth: Where Violence and Nonviolence Meet

We are presented with an interesting tension. Crucifixion is an unambiguously violent practice. It humiliates, denigrates, and reduces the crucified to nothing, robbing the victim first of dignity, then of life itself.[12] Yet it would be hard to characterize the pain of labor and violence done to a woman's body[13] during the birth experience as "violent" according to our present scheme. Giving birth does not normally "hinder Godward transformation." At least in Crysdale's theological report, childbirth is a sacred experience, not unlike baptism or marriage. And this is why the labor metaphor has such power: despite what is happening at a historical level, at the theological level God is transforming human violence into nonviolence. Crucifixion (an inherently violent, damaging, degrading practice) becomes childbirth—a sacred, generative, and transforming kind of suffering. God takes human violence and overcomes it by enduring it.

The necessity of the cross' violence is not a necessity of exchange, nor is it the necessity of exhaustion (that is, exhausting some divine wrath). The labor of God locates the necessity of violence on the cross in its conversion. Under any circumstance other than the birth of a child, what happens to a woman's body in labor would be—like the cross—unambiguously violent. But bringing forth new life, at least on the telling of Crysdale and others, derails the process, makes it sacred, makes the harm a part of the joy. At the cross, God turns violence into its opposite. God does not (or does not only) defang violence, expose it, or exhaust it. By enduring violence and producing new life from it, God-in-Christ converts it.

It is interesting, then, to find that the Scriptures themselves witness divine labor and birth in something like these terms. For example, when we turn to the Gospel of John, we notice that Jesus' response to crucifixion would be more appropriate to the experience of a woman giving birth than to a man being tortured to death. Let us attend to the cries of Jesus on the cross. In John 19:28-30, we read that Jesus "knew that all was now completed" (εἰδὼς ἤδη πάντα τετέλεσται) and, having slaked his thirst on sour wine, said, "It is finished" (τετέλεσται), and then "bowed his head and gave up his Spirit" (κλίνας τὴν κεφαλὴν παρέδωκεν τὸ πνεῦμα). Although it is not the custom for modern translations to append an exclamation point for emphasis, the impulse is not uncommon among commentators. Throughout his recent theological commentary, F. Dale Bruner even uses "It is finished!" as a refrain of sorts, emphasizing the finality and depth of Jesus' ministry as the Logos from the beginning of the Gospel through to the end.[14] For John, the crucifixion begins the exaltation and the glorification of the Logos of God, when Jesus' earthly mission has been completed and his reunification with the Father is imminent. Jesus previews his exaltation at the cross three times in the so-called lifted-up sayings (3:14; 8:28; 12:32); in one of these he conspicuously alludes to Numbers 21:4-9. While speaking to Nicodemus, Jesus compares himself to the bronze serpent lifted on a pole by Moses before the people. Just as the exilic generation knew rescue as they looked upon the hanging serpent, so will the whole world know eternal life as it looks up to the exalted Christ on the cross (John 3:14-16). At the cross, Jesus is physically lifted up in what is meant to be a humiliating public execution. In light of John's language of glory, however, readers know that what is really happening is the inception of Jesus' complete and final victory. If crucifixion is what is happening, Jesus' response is entirely inappropriate. Jesus appears to be engaged in something more like Crysdale's childbirth, where the suffering itself is a part of the exultation. This last shout, declaring that the work is done, sounds to our ears like the laboring woman who sees her travails coming to an end. The gasps and pants, the pains and lasting marks have all been weathered. Success is at hand; something new has been born into the world at last.

But this language is not unique to the New Testament. In fact, John's portrayal of the cross sounds a great deal like the words of the prophet in Isaiah 42:

> The LORD goes forth like a soldier, like a warrior he stirs up his fury; he cries out, he shouts aloud, he shows himself mighty against his foes. *For a long time I have held my peace, I have kept still and restrained myself; now I will cry out like a woman in labor, I will gasp and pant.*[15] I will lay waste mountains and hills, and dry up all their herbage; I will turn the rivers into islands, and dry up the pools. I will lead the blind by a road they do not know, by paths they have not known I will guide them. I will turn the darkness before them into light, the rough places into level ground. These are the things I will do, and I will not forsake them. They shall be turned back and utterly put

to shame—those who trust in carved images, who say to cast images, "You are our gods." (Isaiah 42:13-17 NRSV)

The travail metaphor occurs throughout the Old Testament, the particular form of the simile *kayyōwlēdāh* ("like a woman in labor") alone appearing nine times in the Masoretic Text. The closely related form *yōwlēdāh*, which lacks the prepositional prefix, occurs in the Masoretic Text three times: in Isaiah 21:3, Hosea 13:13, and Micah 5:2. Each instance follows the Masoretic Text's standard convention for *kayyōwlēdāh*: labor is used as a simile predicated of someone or something that is not Israel's God experiencing pain and fear. In only one of the occurrences of *kayyōwlēdāh*, Isaiah 42:14, is the simile predicated of YHWH. If we narrow our focus to Isaiah as it has been canonically received,[16] this explicit use of female imagery to describe God constitutes a strange outlier[17] that encourages us to consider the difference between how God executes divine labors and how we execute ours.

The prophetic and poetic oracles in Isaiah—following standard ancient Near Eastern convention—often treat cities as women and citizens as the city's daughters; female imagery, and therefore metaphorical applications of its semantic associations, widely pepper the Isaianic oracles.[18] A strong emphasis is placed on a woman's ability to bear children (e.g., 7:14; 8:3; 49:20), and some literary mileage is drawn from the pain accompanying labor (13:8; 21:3; 26:17). So what shall we make of this relatively common metaphor's being applied to Israel's God? The use in 42:14 could be unique in that the focus is not so much on the pain of labor as it is on the confident, powerful determination of the one who labors to succeed in giving birth.[19] It also could be that we should focus on the implicit rhetorical relationship that gives God a certain "humanness."[20] In what follows we will review the arguments, ultimately endorsing aspects of both views.

Whatever else can be said, the travail metaphor clearly stands in a secondary position, governed by the controlling image of a mighty warrior.[21] Kathryn Darr capitalizes on this juxtaposition, suggesting that the cry of labor, normally a cipher for intense agony, has been altered to suggest power, confidence, and determination.[22] In the Hebrew Scriptures, *kayyōwlēdāh* is embedded within co-texts where the primary associations with childbirth are fear and pain. So, for example, Psalm 48:4-6 depicts Israel's enemies "in panic" (*nibĕhălû*), "trembling" (*rĕṣādâ*), "like a woman in labor." Isaiah 13:6-8 is similar. Here

Babylon will "be dismayed" (*nibĕhălû*) "like a woman in labor." The four instances in Jeremiah are likewise accompanied by pain and fear: *ḥîl* ("anguish," Jeremiah 6:24); *ḥărādâ* and *paḥad* ("panic and dread," Jeremiah 30:5-6); *wĕrĕṭeṭ, ṣārâ,* and *waḥăbālîm* ("and fear," "distress," "and labor pains," Jeremiah 49:24); on hearing terrifying news, the king of Babylon's hands "fall helpless," and he is overcome with "anguish" (*ḥîl*, Jeremiah 50:43).[23] A survey of the travail simile's use in the Masoretic Text suggests that the instance in Isaiah 42 is doubly unique. It is here applied to Israel's God and surrounded by co-texts that suggest *nothing* of pain or agony. On the contrary, Deutero-Isaiah's oracle depicts God as an implacable soldier in keeping with the warrior-king motif as depicted in Exodus 15:3.

The travail image in Isaiah 42 then—predicated of God and subordinated to the leading warrior metaphor—suggests a different kind of labor pain. We see here a determined woman, equal to the task of birth, controlling her groans to coincide with the strains and pushes of her labor. When we apply the labor metaphor as a model for God, what stands out is not so much what or who God births but how God does so. God will endure labor's pain. But this suffering is not—as C. S. Lewis once remarked—simply to be suffered.[24] Instead the pain is to be channeled, catalyzing success.

Success, confidence, unadulterated joy—these are the marks of God's labor. The trope of God's "humanness" is therefore prescient, for what we see in Isaiah 42 is nothing less than a prolepsis of Jesus' cry at the cross. Victorious, exultant, "thinking nothing of the shame" (αἰσχύνης καταφρονήσας, Hebrews 12:2), Jesus enacts a spiritual birth that is utterly nonviolent. The harm to his body unto death in no way impinges on his Godwardness. It is constitutive of it. Jesus' total enfleshment of divine nature *does*—and, as we shall argue below, *must*—incorporate a certain cost. The destruction of the body that results in spiritual birth is not some unfortunate historical happenstance. It is rather indicative of divine creative genesis from everlasting to everlasting.

God's labor is itself a transforming act: not unmasking scapegoating practices and naming victims, but instead simply converting a brutal human practice, crucifixion, into something that it is not and was never intended to be. The demonic powers sought murder, God allowed them to do it, and then God turned a murder into birth from above. Notice that God's labor preserves the Girardian—and really we should include most species of *Christus Victor*—insistence that the fathers were right: the crucifixion was a trap laid for the forces of evil. The devil and the devil's minions sow violence and reap nonviolence in a spectacular display of God's generative and implacable power. This is because they have put the wrong person on a cross. Rather than eliminating just another prophet, the powers have tried to execute the incarnate Word. If God chooses to make crucifixion childbirth, that is God's prerogative; and if God's prerogative thwarts the best laid plans of the enemy and bears a new, spiritual family, it is our place to marvel and to give thanks.

The Labor of the Passible God

The labor of God provides the epistemic access point necessary for rightly understanding why it is that some violence is necessary for atonement. Two things should be noted. First, and as we have already seen, God's act of deliverance is fundamentally transformative, and part of what is to be transformed is humankind's violent nature. God converts violence into nonviolence by converting a particularly vile form of execution into an act of spiritual genesis. In a way, this already recovers for us a critical aspect of the cross' radicality: the cross marks the moment in human history where God converts violence, transforming it from its intended end into the means by which newness and vitality enter the world. But this does not mean that God repudiates suffering. In fact, the labor of God at the cross does something like the opposite.

Through this first insight into violence-transformed-into-nonviolence, we come to the second insight labor gives us into the reason for Jesus' crucifixion: in a world like the one God created, suffering is the cost of creating newness, and God does not excuse Godself from this experience. More plainly, if God is to give birth, then God will undergo labor just as women do. We have shown that this suffering is nonviolent—that in the present case it actually transforms violence into nonviolence—but it is nevertheless suffering.

In this way, the image of the labor of God at the cross is brought to bear directly on our doctrine of God and, in particular, divine impassibility. The picture we have of God's nonviolent suffering in the atonement must be part and parcel of our notion of God's eternal nature.

And, given the doctrine of divine simplicity, if God is said to have labored at the cross, then God is a laboring God as such: nonviolent suffering has been an aspect of God's nature from eternity or it is a false predicate.

Eberhard Jüngel's *God as the Mystery of the World* is perhaps the twentieth century's most uncompromising *teologia crucis*.[25] Throughout the work, Jüngel targets Descartes, whose god he takes to be the sine qua non of the "god of the philosophers." In Descartes' philosophy, humankind was, for the first time, able to secure the ego apart from any foundation other than the experience of thought from moment to moment. Of course, this is no stable foundation for genuine empirical knowledge, so Descartes offers us an account of the so-called philosopher's god: a god who has no defect, no weakness. God's power secures our power, but, because God's existence is known undoubtedly only "through me" (i.e., through my thought, reflection, etc.), my only access to knowledge of the divine is in radical contradistinction to what I want to posit as the divine essence (namely, infinite omnipresence). This metaphysical method places an impassable gulf between how we know God and what we want to know God to be.

From this point, Jüngel is prepared to press his case by positing the ultimate act of divine address: the Crucified God. Descartes' god of infinite power is set aside in favor of crucifixion, which is "the criterion for any possible concept of God . . . which corresponds to the being of God."[26] Jüngel is influenced by Heidegger here, claiming that God's struggle with nothingness, God's giving "nothingness a place within being," discloses to us in the event of crucifixion "God's endless suffering," which reveals that "God is rather the *one who exists for others*."[27] Jesus' death is the defining act of God, absolutely critical to God's being internally consistent in God's nature.[28] This is because in God's triune Self, the persons of the Trinity are truly "for one another" and in Being-for-the-Son the Father is most truly the Father. However, if one is to be completely for the other, and one fully realizes oneself in that act, then one is constantly self-abnegating. Only God could "localize nothingness within divine being" without being overcome by nothingness and thence nothing. In fact, it is God's endless liberty— God's "self-determination" in Jüngel's verbiage—that could allow such a thing even to be. Theology must be careful, however, not to place the historical particularity—the death of Jesus—before the eternal nature of the divine. To put it another way, God has, from everlasting to ever-lasting, always been in the business of emptying Godself for the sake of the other. This happens eternally in the self-giving communion of the Trinity and is realized in its anthropological fullness in the incarnation and death of the Son.

To say that God is crucified, then, puts theology on an edge. For on the one side of that edge is patripassianism, in which the Father suffered the cross and in which suffering and even death—if some of death-of-God theology is to be heard—is God's eternal nature as such. A gloomy theology, to be sure, and one that fails to account for the confession of the Scriptures and the church that God is the God of the living (e.g., Psalm 42:2; Mark 12:27). But on the other side of that edge is the utterly impassible God so decried by Jüngel and so contrary to the church's proclamation that the Word became flesh, endured all the vagaries of the human condition including its final, inevitable, and irreversible facet, death, and redeemed them in toto.[29] There must be some conceptual discipline that constrains the cross from being suffered by the entire Godhead while nevertheless acknowledging the role of suffering within the divine Being.

On this point, Jürgen Moltmann suggests that the Father suffers not the cross but rather the loss of his Son:

> The rejection expressed in [Jesus'] dying cry, and accurately interpreted by Ps. 22, must therefore be understood strictly as something which took place between Jesus and his Father, and in the other direction between his Father and Jesus, the Son—that is, as something which took place between God and God. The abandonment on the cross which separates the Son from the Father is something which takes place within God himself. . . .[30]

Moltmann's solution is to retain the notion of divine suffering but to locate it differently within the hypostases. So it is that, in light of the notion of labor, the Second Person of the Trinity suffers in physical and spiritual labor while the Father suffers the loss of the newborn's Mother. There is an aspect to divine suffering that is intra-Trinitarian. Just as the incarnation itself marks a kind of divine descent that stretches or pushes against the oneness of the Godhead, so too does the Word's descent into death. The Father loses the Mother but gains the children and, ultimately, in an overcoming of negation itself, recovers the Mother into the union of the Godhead by the binding power of the Spirit. To experience this loss as loss, the loss itself must be real: the labor really must cost this Mother her life. Truly, careful reflection on this point brings us close to incoherence; it is not at all clear how the Godhead can genuinely know the loss of a Person without lapsing into tritheism. It is not wrong to acknowledge that this is mysterious and difficult to parse,[31] but neither is it wrong to confess it as true.

The implication, then, is that the death of God is nothing new, either within God's eternal self or in the history of God's interaction with creation. As we will see below, the Scriptures picture the creation itself as the product of God's eternal self-abnegation. The first birth, as it were, was the cosmos; the second birth was God's spiritual children.[32] Both proceed from God's for-the-other nature, and both involve God's "unity with perishability," as Jüngel terms it. This means, however, that we must read the Genesis creation accounts anew. When God creates through the Logos—that is, when God speaks the world into being—it is through the Son's being-for-the-world that creation takes place (John 1:3). In a sense, this prefigures the incarnation and the cross. The birth of the world, like the birth from above, for lack of a better word, *hurts*.

This pattern is found in several places in the biblical text where God is thought of as giving birth. In Isaiah 42, for example, successful birth results not—as in Isaiah 9:5-6—in a son but in destruction.[33] Some even picture the newborn as a monster in order to preserve the integrity of the metaphor.[34] However far the labor metaphor is pushed, the larger context in Deutero-Isaiah is of a universal cycle of destruction followed by new life and new hope. It might even be that a kind of proto-Marxist anti-imperialism or a proto-Hegelian ideology of universal history undergirds this oracle.[35] Such notions can be entertained because the prophet so clearly emphasizes the necessity of the creative destruction of the old in order to make space and possibility for the new. Whether or not a true zero-sum game lurks in the interstices, we probably cannot say, but we cannot deny that the labor metaphor is present in order to witness to the well-known pattern of destruction-leading-to-creation. At least here, what is new cannot come about but by the creative destruction of what is old. And this destruction, this flattening of the exiles' road, is what God's labor produces.

Jesus' cry at the cross should alert us to a similar point: God is once again accepting the burden of birthing pangs. This time, however, God is clearly the object of the destruction that all genesis requires. Rather than bring forth creative destruction, Jesus undergoes it. If there is a universal history, a cycle of destruction issuing in new birth, it has always been God's burden to bear, and, as we shall see, God has indeed done this sort of thing before. The labor pains of the cross are a novel but thematically consistent economic manifestation of God enduring what is needful to bring about what God wants born.

Moreover, God's actual goal in the Isaianic text bears some consideration. Notice that the end of this promise of rescue from exile is a kind of judgment by shame. Those Israelites who called idols gods will, in the face of the second exodus, be utterly humiliated even as they are redeemed. And, as the labor metaphor implies, the cross is another instantiation of this internal dynamic with spiritual fruits far beyond anything Israel's exiles might have imagined. God's labor—which should be divine humiliation as imperial forces denigrate yet another would-be threat—results ultimately in the humiliation of those demonic powers that thought they were in control. This time it is not only Israelites who are shamed: the world's greatest empire is humiliated by Jesus' conversion of an unequivocally violent structure—crucifixion— into the nonviolent birth of a spiritual people. In the labor of God, the gospel is as dark and jarring as it is hopeful: imperial torment does not become clean or bloodless, but neither does it remain mere torment or accomplish its goals. The labor of God witnesses to new life and the conversion of destruction at the extremes of human suffering.

Creation: The First Labor of God

The Scriptures thus indeed show a God whose creation is accompanied by destruction—destruction in which God's own being participates. And it will therefore come as no surprise that God's first birthing—the creation of the cosmos—bears this same mark. Consider Psalm 90:2:

> Before the mountains were birthed,
>   and you labored with earth and world,
> From age to age,
>   you were there, God.[36]

Scholarly approaches to Psalm 90:2 generally take two different tacks. On the first, the feminine imagery of God birthing the mountains and laboring with the earth and the world is treated as anomalous, perhaps indebted to pagan or preexilic cosmogonic creation myths.[37] Spending time and space in consideration of the uncommon metaphor distracts from the main point of Psalm 90—human frailty and divine permanence—and is thus not worth pursuing other than as a passing point of interest. On the second approach, the imagery is examined and to some extent valorized.[38] It is noted that travail language is theologically scandalous, positing a feminine aspect to the divine nature, militating against notions of divine immutability and impassibility, and at least casting doubt on the classical doctrine of *creatio ex nihilo*. Yet, neither approach treats the metaphor's intrinsic literary function within the psalm as a whole.

Commentators are surely right to assess Psalm 90 as a sober meditation on the fleeting nature of human existence.[39] Our troubles are relentless (v. 10), and yet life as a whole passes quickly (vv. 5-6). Contrast this with divine life that is endless (vv. 2b, 4). The best we can do is spend what little time we have as wisely as possible (v. 12), pray for abundant blessing (vv. 13-16), and trust that an eternal God can extend the legacy of our work beyond the grave (v. 17).

Seeing that the psalm is essentially a reflection on mortality, however, one supposes that language related to birth—the beginning of life—might bear some import. So it is that the psalm sets up an implicit comparison. Like human beings, God gives birth. Like human beings, God has struggled in the process. The difference, suggests the psalmist, is what sort of offspring we bear. Psalm 90 pictures God giving birth to mountains, earth, and the whole cosmos. Human beings, however, bear lives that seem like withering, scorched grass (vv. 5-6). When God gives birth, the offspring *last*. They weather time in much the same way as the divine parent: implacable, eternal, without much notice. We, however, cannot escape the ticking of the clock. Mortality is always before us.[40] This contrast sets up the center of the psalmist's complaint: God does not know what it is like to be chased by death. Without this critical experience, the Creator cannot rightly appreciate what it is like to endure divine wrath (vv. 7-9). Because God is essentially different from us (especially in regard to time and its passage) God does not understand—experientially—what suffering really feels like. The use, then, of *ḥûl* ("writhing in labor") fundamentally *subverts* the psalmist's complaint.

"Writhing in labor" is the last thing we should expect of an implacable, eternal God. If children are said to take on something of the character of the parents, then we must look beyond a mountain's immovability to find the family resemblance. In context, of course, the mountain lasts like the divine parent. And we might note that though mountains last longer than human beings, they too are changed by a multitude of forces. From the vagaries of weather to the grinding of tectonic plates, a mountain's life—like God's—is long, but it is not static.[41] Throughout, the psalm oscillates between meditative reflection on God's lastingness and exuberant acknowledgment of God's unpredictable interactions with the created order, ending with a call for God to repent (*šûb*, v. 13), to relent, to end incessant suffering. The psalm's structure itself mimics the nature of the characters it describes. And this is the decisive import of the labor metaphor in Psalm 90. Though God is "from age to age," when God decides to give birth to the world God does not expect to be excused from the natural course of things: with birth comes pain, struggle, and sometimes loss. God can expect to outlast the destructive forces that accompany creative enterprises, but God is nevertheless willing to undergo them.

Since these texts explicitly connect a sort of divine suffering to the creation of the world, we have good reason to partially endorse readings of the Genesis accounts that incorporate struggle or pain. A number of Old Testament scholars suggest that the *tōhū wābōhû* of Genesis 1:2 refers to something like malignant chaos[42] and that creation was an act of primordial combat through which God is pictured as subduing the chaos to goodness.[43] On this view, Israel's God wrestles with and overcomes chaos, imposing order where before things were "formless and void," to borrow the classic English translation. We say *partially* because, as J. Richard Middleton has argued, whether a combat myth lies behind the first chapter of Genesis, the canonical form of the text clearly depicts God as "encountering no resistance in creating the world."[44] Thus, the final form of the text has been written and/or edited to suppress the regnant ancient creation myths in which "primal evil is a constitutive dimension of the cosmos" and in which constant violence is needed to preserve "the fragile cosmic order imposed by the gods."[45] If the creation account in Genesis 1 is taken as a discrete literary unit, therefore, the final version has been edited in such a way that we cannot really access its tradition history. Put simply, Genesis 1 on its own is no witness to *Chaoskampf.*

That said, it is interesting to note that if an editor has in fact suppressed the vestiges of an original, more violent creation account, then the biblical account could be said to transform the creation violence of accounts like that of the *Enuma Elish* into the nonviolent labor of Israel's God. And this is, of course, what we have already seen the labor of God do to the Roman cross. The themes of the seven-day creation account are startlingly familiar: God is equal to the task at hand; God willingly engages in an act of labor, taking on its inherent difficulties such that God must rest on the last day; and God's generative project requires creative destruction in the form of separation (1:4, 6), shaping (1:2), and divisions (1:9).

Although Genesis does not use the labor metaphor as does Psalm 90:2, bringing it into conversation with other canonical voices is not beyond the pale. Such a reading could open our ears to the themes of creative destruction, suffering that leads to new creation, and God's participation in these experiences. If we read the Genesis account this way, we may be able to gain interpretive purchase on the obscure account of the tree in the garden and what it is to be "like gods." Reading labor into the canonical Genesis account lends it greater interpretive coherence and brings it thematically in line with the theological trajectories we have already sketched.

God creates in Genesis in a way that is analogous to the way God gives birth at the cross. Creation is a challenge, it incurs a cost, but it is nevertheless nonviolent in that coercion is present, but in such a way that the results of coercion are "good." Athanasius writes, "There is thus no inconsistency between creation and salvation, for the One Father has employed the same agent for both works, effecting the salvation of the world through the same Word who made it in the beginning."[46] Of course Athanasius is thinking of the creation through John 1:3, where the Logos is the agent of creation. But we are called to add that the work of the cross and the work of creation, both accomplished through the Son, bear the striking marks of the same fashioner, the same labor, the same God from age to age. Divine travails at creation and cross illuminate the connection between the two actions of the one God and also give good reason to suspect a kind of pathos internal not only to God's acts but also to God's being. Karl Barth's enigmatic doctrine of Jesus Christ as the subject—and not only the object—of election[47] suggests that whatever else we may say, the Godhead "anticipates" the suffering of the cross from eternity. And if the cross is part of election, and its experience is known before the created order, it is also not only a part of God's economy but comprehended in God's immanent nature. This means the following: the economy of God is shaped "Christly" and, therefore, is cruciform.[48] The pattern of the cross—in which labor leads to new life—comprises something of the *Urstruktur* of the cosmos. It is therefore not hard to suggest that cosmic creation itself must share in some of the features of the cross, namely, a kind of labor, work, suffering.

There is interpretive payoff to importing the themes of labor into the Genesis account of creation. Specifically, we may suggest that the so-called curse of Genesis 3:16, in which God tells the woman that the pain of childbirth will "greatly increase" (*'arbe issebônēk*), should be read as Eve in fact receiving the "knowledge of good and evil." The fruit and its blessings are both goods, but one of the tests of the garden is to see whether human beings will receive God's goods on God's terms or on their own.[49] What is on offer at the tree, and what the woman will receive well before she is ready, is exactly what the serpent predicts: being like God. In this case "being like God" involves the extraordinary pain, indeed the threat to one's own life that accompanies genesis. Thus, it is that when God undertakes a last birth at the cross, God acknowledges and recapitulates the now-universal experience of labor, even absorbing the nonbeing of death into Godself.

Likewise, in the garden the man now experiences the vicissitudes of a different kind of labor. God, who has known in God's own creation the diminishing returns of investing labor into human beings, spills out this experience on human men who—often futilely—till the land. The result is a kind of sharing in the divine life, but a sharing that is wholly oppressive. Human beings are not apt to live—in these ways at least—as God lives: without undue suffering or, in keeping with our central theme, violence.

An enduring challenge then is to develop the godly character that imitates God's own power to transform violence into nonviolence, to suffer the pains of birth and the vagaries of the field in such a way as to become more like God rather than less. But surely this is too much to ask of human beings! The man whose luck just does not hold in business, the woman who is horribly disfigured by the ravages of labor—what resources of character do they have to cross from pain, bitterness, and resentment into joy, peace, and, as Crysdale described it, resurrection? In the next chapter, we will look a bit deeper into the nature of second birth and the qualities of life, character, personhood, and spirit that second birth imparts to the God-born. We will see that the labor of the cross was not in vain, that it birthed a new family—a new people with new parents—who share, by birthright and nature, in the divine life.

The Nonviolent Suffering of God as Gospel

As we encounter it in the present, the neoliberal world order reclaims something of the oppressive ubiquity of Rome, governed as it is in and through various applications of the will to power in which people are means not ends, pawns dragooned by impersonal market and imperial forces that, on the Christian telling, are themselves either masks for or puppets of the demonic. In the midst of this dispiriting state of affairs, the proclamation of the cross as the labor of God sounds as it must have sounded out of the mouth of the Lord's first followers: like an actual gospel. Jesus' birth pangs hold within them the promise of new life and new hope and, as part of that project, genuine resistance against the powers. If the God of the universe can convert the cross into childbirth, transform violent subjugation into nonviolent suffering, then what might this God do with those who would be more than data points in the global marketplace or unwilling martyrs to utopian ideals? God's labor shows us that, yes, suffering is built into spiritual regeneration, but it is not the suffering of despair, nor does negation have the last word.

Indeed, resurrection joy is bound up with travail. This is so because the world itself takes its form analogously from the triune God who exists in a constant self-abnegation, existing wholly for the other. Thus, every generative act in which God partakes involves a cost that God willingly bears. In the creation of the cosmos, in the return of the exilic generation, and at the crucifixion of Jesus, the historical expressions of God's being-for-us must be characterized in terms of nonviolent suffering. The hurts and harms that God both bears and inflicts are for others. They aim at conversion, transformation. And what is immanent to

God's being is expressed economically and analogously in the bringing forth of the universe by the labor of the eternal Word. When we see these events as birth pangs, we are able to understand how something as cruel and vicious as the cross is both necessary and transformed. We are also better able to see how the birth from above and the birth of the cosmos are interrelated, acts performed by a self-same God who infuses in creation and redemption a similar structure: labor leads to life. In a strange and wonderful way, we are able to claim that despite the best efforts of a demonic regime, the cross was no more "violent" than the hospital bed of a laboring woman. Bloody, long, and painful? Yes. But also saturated by the joy of new life. In this message the church can once again speak, and speak radically and therefore truly. Once again, from within and against neopagan cultures, the church offers the hope of a new way of being and of believing, once again offering a genuine invitation to respond, to be born again.

4

BIRTHING THE CHURCH
How the Cross Addresses Sin

Of the idiosyncrasies characteristic of contemporary atonement theology, perhaps the most peculiar is that atonement, based as it is on the "at-oneing" of God and humanity, never appears to be concerned with a fundamental change in us. A few examples: What is at stake in penal substitution is the removal of guilt and the meting out of appropriate punishment. This apparently "at-ones" the guilty person and her God, despite the fact that nothing about the cross produces anything in her that might prevent her from accruing more guilt in the future. There are external issues involving God's justice and her violation of it, but, once removed, one would be hard-pressed to come up with a conceptual justification for what Christian theology has classified as sanctification. The sin has been dealt with once and for all; life change, if it matters at all, matters for other reasons. The cross certainly does something to Jesus, but it does not do anything to me. Moral influence schemes fare a bit better here but are still ultimately inert. Yes, God demonstrates his love for us by coming to live with human beings and then suffers unto death to show that love, but, we might ask, "So what?" It is surely good to know that God is so loving; indeed, one supposes that this brings about peace of mind. But peace of mind is not the same thing as bringing human beings and God together. At their best, models built on the wondrous love of God inspire, initiating in hearers the potential—and sometimes even its actualization—for heroic moral effort. How tragic, then, that such effort almost always ends in failure—because nothing about the striver has changed—and, even worse, occasionally in Pelagianism, because the striver has met God's standards on her own merit and individual will. But there are still other possibilities for atonement theology. Models involving some sort of divine victory are revelatory—Christ exposes the powers for what they are—and efficacious—Christ breaks the chains the powers impose on us. But aside from clarifying the state of the world and perhaps clearing out some barriers to certain life patterns, it is again hard to see how this brings union to God and humanity.

In some ways the cross as the labor of God is a work of protest—protest against every proclamation of the cross that concedes the church's increasing irrelevance by ratifying the status quo in which hearts remain unmarked and unturned and unchanged in the face of the crucifixion of the Son of God. What does the cross accomplish? What does it gain? What life is born from the cries of birth and their accompanying scars? The framing of the question itself points us in the direction of the answer: the divine labor creates new life, new people who bear the nature not of earthly parents but of the true fathering and mothering God. The cross creates a new race, a different sort of people with different blood, different parents, different DNA, even a brand-new extended family. And this matters for atonement theology because it gives a robust answer to the question of how the cross deals with sin. Penal substitution and satisfaction, for example, give fine accounts for how the cross removes a bone of contention between us and God, but they do not explain how the cross renews us. That is to say, they do not connect the sufferings of Christ to a new nature or a new life. Properly speaking, that job belongs to somebody else, the Holy Spirit perhaps.

And this would be an agreeable state of affairs if the post-Christian West were not bursting at the seams with a teeming agglomeration of the walking dead, the sick-unto-death, the corrupted and corrupting children of Sin. More is needed than a clean slate before God; what is needed is an antidote to a plague, a putting together of what has been fractured and broken apart, a neoteric nature composed of wholeness and vitality. That is to say, a new birth.

Sin: More than a Guilt Problem

Delivering an atonement theology adequate to this task first demands a better accounting of the task itself. Sin, long deemed the rampant human practice of missing the mark of perfection by an agent's mis-application of her libertarian free will, must be reanalyzed in light of biblical and theological concerns. Attempting something of this task, Ian McFarland writes:

> Though sin may not be within one's direct control, the fact that it is a matter of damaged or distorted relationship means that the sinner cannot dissociate herself from the situation as a purely passive victim of circumstances. On the contrary, moving to the context of relationship in analyzing sin subverts any simple bina-rism according to which responsibility is assessed solely in terms of whether or not the sin was intentional. A person's responsibil-ity is not dependent on the ability to exercise conscious control over her thoughts and actions, but rather derives from that fact that her agency cannot be abstracted from the network of inter-personal relationships in which she participates.[1]

Writing from within the Lutheran tradition, McFarland is keen to retain a doctrine of universal, original sin in humanity—the sinner is not "a purely passive victim"—but McFarland is nevertheless also confronted with the weight of biblical scholarship that has firmly rejected the reduction of sin to something like the individual's willing against the law(s) of God. Whatever sin may be, it is not only something that issues solely from an autonomous agent's decisions. For indeed, if menstruation—which is certainly not a product of the will—is some-thing that needs atonement (Leviticus 15:30; cf. 12:7), then sin must be something larger than intentional violations of a code of law. It is instead a part of "one organic continuum."[2] There is a divine vision for how the world is and ought to be, but "[a]cts of 'awon [sin, iniquity] twist and pervert reality."[3] Sin is something like a force, distorting our perceptions such that even to speak of a "choice" to sin is already to have claimed ground without warrant. This is so because an act of sin alters the judgment; it distorts the right workings of the mind. Isa-iah 5:18-20 illustrates the point. Here, the prophet accuses wayward Israelites "who drag sin ['awon] with cords of falsehood," of "call[ing] evil good and good evil." As sin pervades a life, it results in a skewed perspective, an inability to judge rightly between good and evil. And of course this leads to a second problem: sin may very well be totally unintentional. To the one caught up in sin, to the one who discerns good as evil and vice versa, actions that are intended to be pious may be nothing of the sort.[4]

Dietrich Bonhoeffer takes up something of this theme. He writes, "But man cannot be rid of his origin. Instead of knowing himself in the origin of God, he must now know himself as an origin. He interprets himself according to his possibilities, his possibilities of being good or evil, and he therefore conceives himself to be the origin of good and evil. *Eritis sicut deus*."[5] By "origin" (*Ursprung*) Bonhoeffer does not only mean that human beings come from God or bear God's image. Thinking here with Karl Barth, Bonhoeffer indicts the human movement in which a person replaces God as the all-determining determinant with herself. The horizons of possibility for one's existence then no longer issue from the nature and character of God; they are instead supplanted by human will, and, lest we accuse him of falling into the individualism he so often rejects, we remember that for Bonhoeffer "man is an indivisible whole, not only as an individual in his person and work but also as a member of the community of men and creatures in which he stands." Meditating further on this whole, Bonhoeffer suggests that "this reality which is founded on God and apprehended in Him, is what the question of good has in view."[6] We want to suggest that the converse of the "question of good" is the question of evil: in biblical terms, sin. But notice how something like the doctrine of illumination is implicated in the very notion of right action: the right reality itself is only known in the knowledge of God. We approach paradox, for right action depends on a right sense of what is, but a right sense of what is depends on a right relation with God, which cannot be known without a right sense of what is. As with Barth, Bonhoeffer depends wholly on an invading grace that sets the mind aright such that the good is done.[7] And wherever this grace is absent, an inescapable system of sin reigns. For if even the knowledge of good and evil is itself corrupted—for to have it sans God is not, properly speaking, to have it at all—then one wonders if "the good" so conceived is the good in fact.

This is all to say that Bonhoeffer's dictum that one "cannot be rid of [one's] origin" is theologically fraught. Human thought and action must proceed from somewhere, and there appear to be only two possibilities. In the first, reality is apprehended by and in God; in the second, human beings are, to borrow the parlance of Western individualism, self-determining. But self-determination itself is at best a misleading concept for, as we have already seen, the individual is mired in misperception, enmeshed in an equally misperceiving community, and, referring back once more to McFarland's caveat, "cannot be abstracted from the network" of either.

Nor should we mistake any of this as philosophical abstraction: the Scriptures almost uniformly push against the notion that sin is something rational agents elect in a vacuum. Consider the passion of Paul, who in Romans 7:19 cries out as Israel-sans-Christ: "For I do not do the good I want, but the evil I do not want is what I do" (NRSV). Paul here gives voice to Israel's particular experience of the Adamic condition, albeit analyzed from the perspective of one who has, as we will note below, been born of God.[8] Reflecting on the tenor of Paul's thought, consider the Community Rule from Qumran, where we read, "My mistakes ['awon], transgressions, sins, together with the corruption of my heart, belong to the counsel of the rotten and to the ones who walk in darkness. For no one [sets] her [own] road, no one establishes her [own] steps . . ." (1QS 11:9-10a).[9] To put it another way, Paul gives voice to what humanity in general and Israel in particular has universally felt: sin or sinfulness is something powerful and has the characteristic of agency. It is not merely an action not in keeping with what God wants done; sin is active. So it is, then, that Paul can claim that "through one man sin entered the world" (Romans 5:12a) because sin exercises a kind of power in concert with or through human agency. It may be that "sin" should be replaced by "Sin," because the powers appear to be in play.[10] Alternatively, but along the same lines, it might be that "sin" in Romans 7 is a personification of the serpent in Genesis 3, such that each time Paul uses ἁμαρτία, we may read the story of Adam and Eve's temptation, applying all the cunning of the serpent to the force of ἁμαρτία. Thus, "Sin (the serpent) was lurking in the garden prior to man's fall, but had found no opportunity to attack man until the commandment, 'You shall not eat of it' (Gen 2:17) had been given."[11]

Thus, despite the focus of much of atonement theology, the biblical and theological vision of sin bears little resemblance to crude forensic interpretations. Even if we concede that lawbreaking is implicated as a part of our hamartiology, it simply cannot be comprehensive or even the critical core. The Scriptures portray sin as much more than an individual's decision to violate this or that command of God. Sin enmeshes, mires, attacks, lurks, deceives, confounds, blinds, and, ultimately, kills—and these are not verbs describing actions rationally elected by autonomous agents to perform or not perform. Sin deserves an argot more exacting, more faithful in its description.[12]

A theological and biblical notion of sin therefore inveighs against any conception of atonement that does nothing to address the critical problems that sin actually poses in the real world. At the macro level, sin or sinfulness is "an offense against a divinely ordered norm."[13] While God will not hesitate to punish when it is warranted, God's interests do not primarily lie in punishing those who have disordered what God has ordered. Instead, the Old Testament consistently and pervasively depicts God developing a myriad of different strategies to actually remedy the situation. When we say "situation" we do not mean only the issue of dealing with an individual's infraction, or, as the case may be, accidental impurity. Rather, the "situation" involves the entire community of God, the world, and the way that disorder must be righted, prevented, or expunged. A remedy might include the destruction of a polluting element (as in, e.g., Leviticus 10:1-2) or the sending of a prophet to set the people back on course before exile becomes necessary (e.g., Jeremiah 1:7-10). The goal of God's action is a lasting remedy, "an inner transformation of the heart in order to pursue righteousness rather than sin."[14]

If remedying the sin problem does in fact characterize the nature of God's reaction to human sinfulness, then whatever else it must do, the doctrine of atonement—the "at-oneing" of God and humanity in and through the cross—must show how the crucifixion of Jesus puts the entire human situation to rights. Failing to do so means coterminously failing to keep atonement true to the hamartiology of the Old Testament. The same argument could be made for the New Testament. After all, the expunging of Ananias and Sapphira from the early church community in Acts 5 appears to continue the theme of purifying the community by destruction/removal. If anything, Luke's inclusion of this story confirms that God has not fundamentally altered God's response to sin: if sin not only transgresses and violates but also disorders, then the requisite remedy is meant to restore the divinely ordained order of the world.[15] To put the point more forcefully, God's interests as they are embedded in Torah simply go unserved by an account of atonement that does not explain how the cross directly changes human beings, institutions, and associations. Legal justification is no doubt important, but it is not what is at stake when God worries about the corruption that sin brings to communities. What is needed is not a scapegoat for the guilt sin has incurred—though that might also be required in some cases—but a solution to the problems sin has wrought. Atonement theology ought to account for how it is that the cross of Christ not only rectifies but also remedies sin and its effects. Removing legal condemnation, restoring God's honor, even disarming and unmasking the ultimate weapon of demonic persecution—none of these models of atonement credibly treat the cross as a remedy for sin, for in none of them is the suffering of the cross effecting a transformation in which human beings receive the goal of God's atoning activity. The clean heart of Psalm 51 is more than the clean slate of imputed juridical righteousness.

The reason for this is that, as we have seen, juridical conceptions of sin—or, more broadly, conceptions of sin that characterize it as primarily about the relations between God and human beings—do not adequately account for sin's systemic and insidious nature. A more biblically and theologically faithful doctrine of atonement must be able to address a robust hamartiology. This is to say, it must offer a remedy to the widespread effects of sin and the invidious systems by which sin is sustained.

The present cultural moment in the West is one of profound decay. From a classical perspective, the disordering of loves has been so complete that institutional and communal corruption is rife, nigh ubiquitous. Such a moment cries out for radical and systemic reordering—the sort of response the message of the cross once commanded and, we believe, can command again. The gospel simply cannot be either good or news unless it can do more than pronounce a favorable verdict between God and me as I sit in the dock. As the reader will surely already have surmised, a theology of the cross must be a theology of rebirth. As we will now see, the New Testament image of rebirth—the birth that proceeds from the labor of God on the cross—provides an entrée into just such an account.

Rebirth in Titus 3: New Parents, New Family, New Inheritance

As the scholarly appellation indicates, the theological content in the pastoral epistles skews in the direction of the practical concerns of ecclesiology. So, for example, the very beginning of the letter to Titus addresses qualifications for those who would order and protect the church (ch. 1); the discourse subsequently turns to issues of conduct among the assembled (ch. 2). The theological rationale for this advice—or at least the ecclesiological-salvific vision that undergirds it—is brought to the fore in the third chapter to explain why it is that Christian conduct is expected to rise above the licentiousness that characterizes pagan life patterns. We should at this point not be surprised to find that the author seizes on the language of a transformative, spiritual rebirth:

> But when the goodness and loving kindness of God our Savior appeared, he saved us, not because of any works of righteousness that we had done, but according to his mercy, through the washing[16] of rebirth and renewal by the Holy Spirit. This Spirit he poured out on us richly through Jesus Christ our Savior, so that, having been justified by his grace, we might become heirs according to the hope of eternal life. (Titus 3:4-7 NRSV)

This section is particularly interesting for its echoes of Spirit-texts from the Old Testament, primarily a catena of texts from the Septuagint's rendering of Ezekiel 36–39.[17] For our purposes, the crucial phrasing comes in Titus 2:14c, where the NRSV has "and purify for himself a people of his own" (καὶ καθαρίσῃ ἑαυτῷ λαὸν περιούσιον). Here the writer weaves in snippets of Ezekiel 37:23, 36:25, and 36:28.[18] We will look at each in turn (the translations that follow are my own).

> Ezekiel 37:23b: I will cleanse them and they will be to me a people and I the Lord will be God to them (καὶ καθαριῶ αὐτούς καὶ ἔσονταί μοι εἰς λαόν καὶ ἐγὼ κύριος ἔσομαι αὐτοῖς εἰς θεόν).

> Ezekiel 36:25: I will sprinkle clean water upon you, and you will be clean from all your uncleannesses, and also from all your idols I will cleanse you (καὶ ῥανῶ ἐφ᾽ ὑμᾶς ὕδωρ καθαρόν καὶ καθαρισθήσεσθε ἀπὸ πασῶν τῶν ἀκαθαρσιῶν ὑμῶν καὶ ἀπὸ πάντων τῶν εἰδώλων ὑμῶν καὶ καθαριῶ ὑμᾶς).

> Ezekiel 36:28b: Then you will be a people to me and I will be God to you (καὶ ἔσεσθέ μοι εἰς λαόν κἀγὼ ἔσομαι ὑμῖν εἰς θεόν).

The prophet addresses the defilement accompanying idolatry and the subsequent purification required for what Philip Towner calls "the event of 'becoming' God's people and the ongoing act of 'being' God's people by way of the Godward covenant commitments required of his people."[19] The scare quotes are telling, signaling that in the context of Ezekiel the people are already "God's people." They have already been chosen, rescued, and set apart. What is wanted is the reinstatement of their covenant commitment. The question is whether the same holds true for the Cretan Christians targeted in Titus. Is the Spirit language in Titus 3 channeling the language of Ezekiel to explain or reduce the advent of the Spirit to a kind of eschatological empowerment, or is it something more? The question presses on the Cretan Christians because it bears on what, exactly, the crucifixion of the Messiah accomplished. A change of status? Inspiration that results in "Spirit-generated fulfillment of Torah"?[20] Perhaps the author of Titus—and the prophet too—expect a new ontology, an actual, real change in people, what soul-theorists might have once deemed union to the divine nature. Consider the language of, for example, Ezekiel 36:26-27:

> I will give you a new heart and I will put in you a new spirit. Also I will take out of your body a heart of stone and give you a heart of flesh. I will then put my spirit within you, and I will make (ποιήσω) it such that you follow my statutes and carefully keep my laws. (author translation)

Surely this language indicates something more than inspiration, status change, or empowerment. The introduction of a new spirit, of God's Spirit, does not result in a renewed ability to observe Torah. It is God, acting through a new heart and a new spirit, who conforms Israel to Torah. God does not motivate Israel for a challenging task; God gives Israel new parts, members adequate to the pattern of life set out in Torah, the life of holiness. This is the language of essential change, drastic transformation. And lest we be accused of quibbling here, we are not denying the ethical thrust of Titus 3. Holy living is absolutely in view. The question is where ethical living comes from and if we are to encounter Titus as poetry whose metaphors are meant to be reduced to ornament. Because if not, then we risk taking Titus (and the cross) quite seriously, expecting it to really, actually *do* something quite radical *to us*. Titus, following the spirit—if we may put it that way—of the prophet, speaks of a fundamental change (e.g., a heart of stone exchanged for a heart of flesh), a change in nature or, as we will argue shortly, parentage and—in modern parlance—neural restructuring, rather than a sense of inspiration that ebbs and flows and results in a kind of desultory moral effort. Conflating "rebirth" and "renewal" in Titus 3:5,[21] such that all that is being claimed is a status change from dirty to clean in the eyes of God, not only fails to take "rebirth" seriously; it also denatures the prophetic oracles from which rebirth and renewal have been drawn, peeling back the layers of Ezekiel's genuine-sounding eschatological hope and discovering nothing but theological fantasy underneath. The Christian hope of the cross in the letter to the Christians in Crete is not just an alteration of status from unjustified to justified.[22] Genuinely accounting for the language in the New Testament letter and the Old Testament texts it echoes requires that we take the metaphor of rebirth—and the Spirit's role in that rebirth—seriously.

Pressing this case, consider the Old Testament echoes in Titus 3:4-7. First, we hear in Titus 3:5 an echo of Psalm 104:30 (103:30 LXX, author translation): "You will send out your spirit and they will be created; and you will renew the face of the earth" (ἐξαποστελεῖς τὸ πνεῦμά σου καὶ κτισθήσονται καὶ ἀνακαινιεῖς τὸ πρόσωπον τῆς γῆς).[23] Psalm 104 meditates on the intersection between God's cosmic power to create and sustain and how this is experienced locally by his chosen people. Psalm 104 is cosmic in scope: all of creation renewal is known by us as movements of new life and the wandering presence of God's spirit. Winds, mountains, animals, seasons, even darkness and light, and of course human beings—all are at the mercy of God's provision. When God hides the divine face (104:29), there is death and deprivation. The opposite of this withdrawal of divine favor is the sending of the spirit, accompanied as it is by creation and renewed fruitfulness (104:30). Psalm 104 thus witnesses to the ebb and flow of death and life, destruction and creation, decay and renewal. It is God's choice to send the spirit, to step in, to alter the course of a dying or deprived creation. And, as the psalmist attests, God does not always do this. Sometimes the divine face is hidden. Sometimes the lion finds no prey; sometimes work has no benefit. The norm, as it were, is a generous God with an open hand (104:28), a God who sends his spirit freely into the world to create, sustain, renew.

In the context of Ezekiel 36–39, the echo of Psalm 104 in Titus 3 pictures a dramatic action of the Creator Spirit. The same cosmic creation that generates mountains, hills, and leviathan is experienced by human beings in the church, and it is named "rebirth." Moltmann's interpretation of Psalm 104:29-30 does more than pay lip service to the Spirit's generative and sustaining activities:

> From the continual inflow of the divine Spirit (*ruach*) created things are formed (*bara*). They exist in the Spirit, and they are "renewed" (*hadash*) through the Spirit. This presupposes that God always creates through and in the power of his Spirit, and that the presence of his Spirit therefore conditions the potentiality and realities of his creation.[24]

Moltmann's insight concerning potentiality and reality suggests that when the church describes the Spirit's manifestation, she must call it "rebirth" because only the divine metaphor can account for the experience of potential and reality that has been unleashed. This potential and reality follows in Titus 3:7 where the ultimate end of the Spirit's work is revealed: inheritance ("so that we might become heirs"). Rebirth means a new divine parent, a new divine household, a new spiritual family, and, as befits a natural child, an inheritance.

Paul in Romans 8 works with the same metaphor in the same way. He tells us that those who are "led by the Spirit are children of God" (Romans 8:14), but he does not leave the metaphor alone. He extrapolates, using the model of a parent/child relationship to continue his argument, claiming, "if children, then heirs, heirs of God and joint heirs with Christ" (8:17 NRSV). The parent/child relationship holding between Paul's brothers and sisters and God results in eschatological inheritance and ontological glory (8:17-21). In other words, Paul has more in mind than literary ornament when he conceptualizes us as God's children. The child is indeed like the Father, but the family resemblance, as it were, is predicated not just on the performance of a particular set of actions but on a change that has taken place at the ontological level.

Similar conclusions follow from the echoes of Joel 2:28-29 in Titus 3:6:

> And after these things I will pour out my spirit (ἐκχεῶ ἀπὸ τοῦ πνεύματός μου) on all flesh; your sons and your daughters will prophesy, your aged will dream dreams, and your young will see visions. In these days I will pour out my spirit (ἐκχεῶ ἀπὸ τοῦ πνεύματός μου) even on male and female slaves. (author translation)

Like Psalm 104, Joel 2 juxtaposes God's cosmic creative and sustaining work along with the promise of a local manifestation, in this case
prophecy, dreams, and visions that accompany a Spirit poured out. The
presence of God with the people is accompanied by the traditional acts
of creation and sustaining of creation: rain, fertile soil, abundant crops
(Joel 2:21-24). And, just as in Psalm 104, this is experienced by the
people in a work of the Spirit. Titus 3 seizes on this pattern to explain
that, by the Spirit, the community has experienced spiritual rebirth,
accompanied by a new parent, a new family, and a new inheritance.
The potential to be a divine heir is realized only in the reality of spiritual rebirth.

God's saving activity entails more than a change of status; it entails
an entirely new identity. By bearing spiritual children and heirs, God
has fundamentally changed the Cretan Christians' DNA. Heroic holiness is not something that happens because the Holy Spirit gives the
community greater strength, although that may be the case; holiness is
simply a reflection of who they are. Having been born spiritually, the
spiritual nature is, in its most natural state, a doer of good works (Titus
3:8, 14; cf. Romans 8:1-10: "living by the Spirit"). In this sense the birth
metaphor does carry some of the "like Father, like daughter" declara-
tions so commonly used to explain familial resemblance. Children in
this family are disposed to act this way. It is just the case that our people are like that. The ethical problem, then, is an issue of family, or as
we shall argue below, ecclesiology: the community is not living in light
of what has transpired in their spiritual rebirth.[25]

God's Seed, God's DNA in 1 John 3

In 1 John 3 we see further evidence of ontological transformation, a
second birth into a different family. In what follows, we will argue that
that change is best understood metaphorically as DNA change, and
truly instantiated in the neural substrates of thought and action, such
that Word and Spirit do in fact replace Ezekiel's hearts of stone with
hearts of flesh. The epistle of 1 John 3:9 declares that the God-born
(ὁ γεγεννημένος ἐκ τοῦ θεοῦ) do not sin because God's seed (σπέρμα)
remains within them. No consensus has emerged regarding the use
of σπέρμα in this text, though most proposals share much more than
the rhetoric might indicate.[26] Suggestions include reading σπέρμα as
Spirit, Word, divine nature, and offspring. One might be forgiven for

noting that all of these are highly symbolic and highly interrelated in the Johannine corpus and not worth finely distinguishing. Nevertheless, commentators have a tendency to reduce the argument to endorsing one out of the four possibilities, as if semantic fields operated as nonporous domains of static meaning. To demonstrate what we mean, consider the implications of choosing "offspring." Within the Johannine corpus as a whole, being born of God must still involve somehow receiving a spiritual family heritage as the result of the Son's glorification. Being born of God will still involve having the "word of God abide in you" (1 John 2:14). And, as in John 3, being the child of divine birth still includes the change in family required of those who would see and enter the kingdom of God. If it does not carry these associations, then the text deconstructs to tautology ("Those born of God do not sin because God's children remain in him; they cannot sin because they are born of God").[27] In this case, at least, we would do well to skirt hard-and-fast distinctions. Whether 1 John espouses a protognostic concept of divinization by possession of a divine seed[28] or is meant to be a Johannine sobriquet for the Spirit,[29] or something else entirely, we are best served by respecting the Johannine penchant for highly associative language and supposing that, indirectly at least, all the suggestions are implicated.

We do well, however, to plant the flag on one issue: however we read "seed," it must indicate a particular kind of character, namely, the character of the Father. The logical force of the argument hinges on the fact that being God-born means having God's seed, and, whatever that seed is ontologically, it results in a particular kind of acting in the world.[30] The action is familial; because God is the Father, the children of the Father take on his character. To ears attuned to scientific advances in genetics, the meaning is clear: those born from God share God's DNA.[31] According to John, the God-born live in a world where sin is abolished, the Spirit is present, and the community ethic is or is being purified (1 John 3:10). In short, the people who obey the Word, who have been born of water and Spirit, who have seen and entered the kingdom of God, are now truly the children of God. They have been transformed.

It is helpful to collapse several of these distinctions, to suggest that "both water and Spirit mean 'life'" and that being born of such "becomes simply the writer's way of defining the 'kingdom of God' as 'life' or 'eternal life.'"[32] Two worlds are colliding in a profound manner. Jesus proclaims that God's kingdom is "not from this world" (οὐκ ἔστιν ἐκ τοῦ κόσμου τούτου), but this does not mean that it does not invade this world. In John, of course, this is the whole point. The coming of the Son to live with us results in our being born of God and thereby participating in his kingdom's life (John 1:12-14); the "above" and "below" are united.

Taken together, the passages in Titus and 1 John suggest that in spiritual birth, God has transformed human hearts. God has not only removed sin; God has remedied it and its effects. God has done so by addressing the nature of sin itself. Sin, present in human hearts and human communities, cannot be escaped without new hearts and new communities, without new DNA and a new family.

Rebirth as Ontological Change: Neural Networks, Conversion, and Ecclesiology

Spiritual birth is best described in the following manner: At the cross, Christ labors to bear spiritual children, replacing minds corrupted and hollowed out by sin with minds that firmly and completely grasp their true origin. Christ extricates them out of corrupt familial webs, systems of relationships wholly mired in spiritual blindness, birthing them into a new family, God's family, the church. In what follows, we try to make sense of what it means for faith to produce ontological change. As Christian theology ventures out from the safe confines of classical dualism, it becomes ever more critical to show how it is that the cross does in fact effect change. If spiritual birth "changes our DNA," it is worth pushing to see how much of the metaphor we can map onto the realities we encounter in the sciences.

Of course one's genetic code is not magically rewritten at the moment of faith. It does change over time, however, as do the connections and patterns in neural networks. As we seek to describe the ontological change that comes about in new birth through the labor of the cross, we may begin by turning to the recent findings in the neurosciences. The neurosciences are in the midst of something of a technological renaissance as new and better fMRI becomes available and thus neural networks become more visible. Because of this we expect that some of the present lines of thought will expand and sharpen over time, though we also expect that the overall trajectory will remain mostly stable.

With respect to proclivities and patterns of thought, François Ansermet and Pierre Magistretti write, concerning neural plasticity, "What is determined on the synchronic level is perhaps not fully determined on the diachronic level, that is, in the successive concatenation of traces with one another. From one reworking to the next, the variability of responses increases, distancing the person from his determinants."[33] The suggestion is that proclivities and patterns of thought are not fixed. Successive iterations, in conjunction with experiences and successive reflection, open up new possibilities for thought and action. In our terms, then, new birth by faith will be instantiated in altered neural networks, with new possibilities for thought and action opened up by one's spiritual rebirth. To say that we have "new DNA" is really to carry the birth metaphor into ontology: neural substrates will be implicated in and through conversion, such that new life and new life patterns become possible through religious faith.[34] To put it bluntly, conversion or birth from above is just a massive neural realignment, and that realignment makes a new kind of experience of life possible.

If rebirth through faith opens up new possibilities and proclivities, however, they are only operative from within embeddedness in a new family. For Christians, of course, "new family" is shorthand for "the church" and therefore ecclesiology. What might the neurosciences have to say about social connectedness and family that would be relevant here? At the ground level, what is it that the church does to us (and vice versa)? With respect to familial obligations, recent research implicates mirror neurons in the internalization of the intentional states of others in children as early as seven months old.[35] Thus, the development of a notion of "self" appears to occur simultaneously with one's development of a notion of the other. The two are interconnected and only distinguished in later stages of development. The research shows that children with Autism Spectrum Disorder (ASD), who appear to lack the mirror neurons in question, are "able to recognize what the actor was doing . . . but failed to recognize why the actor was doing it."[36] Given that in most cases it is the family unit within which the brain develops, a strong notion of the self as bound up with these particular others is not hard to imagine. The New Testament both assumes and commands a communal life of faith; these findings help to illuminate why that is.

From a systematic perspective, the labor of God shows why it is that the doctrine of ecclesiology is sourced in the doctrine of atonement. Because the labor of the cross leads to birth, birth indicates family, and, for Christians, family is the church; the first "ecclesiogenesis," to borrow Leonardo Boff's neologism, takes place when the blood and water pour out of Jesus' side. A new, divine family just is produced by the cross. As with one's family of origin, the church is a necessary feature of life if one is to live out one's new potential and proclivities because the family is the place where particular character traits, actions, and ideas are generated, reinforced, and policed. As the God-born increasingly identify as part of a family of faith, novel neural possibilities get selected and hardened, such that, to slip back into the metaphor, the divine DNA gets expressed in life and character.

Just as God labored with the mountains, so Jesus labors with the church. For this reason the Syriac church knew the Holy Spirit as the "Mother of the Church," because in Jesus' death a new creation is being brought about, one in which the old patterns of thought (Romans 12:2), the old familial obligations (Luke 8:21), and the old proclivities are erased and replaced. Transformed hearts and communities make it possible to have sin and its effects remedied, and transformed hearts and communities are made possible because God chooses to enact a new birth, the birth from above, the spiritual rebirth. As atonement, labor makes better sense of how God addresses the biblical notion of sin. Rather than dying in our place, God in Christ labors to give us birth. On this model Jesus' death in childbirth is an exclamation point: even if it costs everything, God will see these children born. In so doing, God unleashes on a blinded and corrupted world fresh possibilities as people with God's DNA live and act as God lives and acts, reflecting God's character by nature rather than by adherence to a code, acting God's acts in keeping with natural proclivities rather than heroic feats of self-will. This is possible because they are born into a new family—the church—one that has already become inured to the divine life such that it can foster the newly God-born, instantiating the divine life as an example and a spur. These people live by the Spirit because they have been born by the Spirit through the agony of the cross.

5

TRANSCENDING EXCHANGE
How the Family of God Gives Up the Gift

The role of the cross in atonement is, on many objective models, like some versions of *Christus Victor*, satisfaction, and penal substitution: conceptually coherent, but only at the macro level. Taking penal substitution as an example, if sin is a crime of infinite magnitude against God, and the penalty for such a crime is death, and it is further the case that God's justice must be met, then, well, somebody must die. This is straightforward explanation; it appeals to minds attuned to something like the systems of justice developed in the West. If a law is transgressed, there must be punishment. A capital crime demands capital punishment. It is at this point, of course, that the actual story of Jesus of Nazareth muddies the waters. For example, why should God accept this man's death for some other person's crimes?[1] It would be as if a convicted murderer sat in the dock while an innocent child walked into the courtroom, declared that she would accept the killer's punishment that he might go free, and the judge decided that this was an acceptable outcome to the case.

Stephen Finlan notes that penal substitution "rarely functions alone; usually it is linked with one or another of the other metaphors."[2] In order to make penal substitution work conceptually—so that it does not appear as absurd as our story about the child executed in a murderer's stead—Christian doctrine conflates the narrative of penal substitution with the practice of sacrifice. Both systems are operative and somehow intertwined. The judge/priest both condemns the murderer and accepts the child as a scapegoat of sorts. What is doubly strange about this intertwining—leaving aside its bizarre entangling of separate systems found in the Old Testament—is that it egregiously lets the condemned get away with murder, offers no account of whether the child's sacrifice will change the criminal's character in any way, and puts an innocent to death for no reason at all. The logic of scapegoating sits in the background, as it were, working but remaining unexpressed.

In effect, Christian doctrine pieces together a kind of theological Frankenstein's Monster, where the logical members of one story or another, or the elements of various Hebrew sacrificial ceremonies, are grafted together in a grotesque amalgamation, a doppelganger of a coherent notion of atonement.[3] To reconstruct the process conceptually, consider again the two stories we have already told. In the first, an innocent child offers to take the sentence due the murderer. Of course it would be absurd for any judge to take the young one up on her offer—unless the court existed within a culture that practiced ritual child sacrifice or scapegoating. And here the sacrificial story comes into play. In this case the child, appealing to legally recognized structures of ritual substitution, may mercifully remove the murderer's offense. The logic of sacrifice rescues the logic of penal substitution from collapsing in on itself but has the unfortunate corollary of creating a bizarre, piecemeal metaphorical universe, one that bears little resemblance to the biblical worlds from which it has been fashioned.

To speak, then, of a penal substitutionary or sacrificial "model" is conceptual farce. We have already seen that the images and metaphors in religious language take on something of the character of scientific models.[4] A faithful image is one that, when extended conceptually, clarifies or suggests how this or that aspect of the religious might be analogous to this or that feature of the image. Now, we should grant that no model will be exhaustive. One supposes that any model claiming this kind of categorical explanatory power should automatically self-invalidate, since the divine cannot be summed or conceptually owned by intellect. That said, we are surely justified in expecting any particular image or model to be coherent, both offering a compelling theological logic for the cross and easily mapping onto the basic historical narrative offered in the Gospels. And as we have just seen, it is demonstrably the case that substitution and sacrifice do not. Why?

First, it should be noted that we have been dealing thus far with *objective* models of atonement. Sacrifice, substitution, ransom: these models posit that something has taken place ontologically, that a barrier between humanity and God was in fact present and that at the cross it was truly and once and for all removed. At the theological level, objective models of atonement are based on a logic of exchange. This for that, him for us, they present the death of Jesus as "for us" in the sense that his life buys ours, or he is taken hostage that we might be released, or he endures punishment meant for us, or he satisfies God's honor or justice or righteousness on our behalf. But to work, in order to feature genuine logical consistency, these models turn out mosaical, fashioned from this scrap of Scripture, that Deuteronomic logic, and this prevailing assumption about God's nature, and this to their philosophical detriment, for they cannot bear genuine conceptual analysis. Some might therefore simply wish to abandon objective models of atonement altogether; there are, after all, subjective versions that might do justice to Scripture and intellectual honesty.

Unfortunately, models that explicitly eschew economies of exchange—that is, subjective accounts—have a hard time making sense of the cross. Consider, for a moment, moral influence models. In these the life of Jesus is primarily instructive, the divine Logos made flesh, instantiating the perfection of the law in a human life. Such a view maps easily onto the Gospel narratives: Jesus' liberative practices and authoritative interpretations of the Torah concretize the notion of a life conformed to the character and purposes of God. But such a view has difficulty making sense of his death as "for us."[5] Perhaps in some ways Jesus models dying well, or takes the practice of nonviolence to its logical conclusion, or shows humanity what and who the powers really are, but the cross does not "do" anything other than make the hope of resurrection really important—for without it who would act as this man did, spitting in the eye of the powers, practically begging them to bring the sword to bear? On views like these, the cross is the exclamation point appended to the sentence that is Jesus' ministry: the life of God lived out in a powers-dominated world like ours ends one way, and that end is grisly. In certain iterations they possess undeniable power, but said power is rhetorical only, truly inspiring moral effort but not providing the ontological and theological grounds for confidence that such effort will have any, to say nothing of lasting, success. In short, subjective models like moral influence hamstring any conviction that faith—simple, unaided trust—in the Christ of the cross can truly *do* anything to human beings, God, or the relations holding between the two, and this in spite of the gospel proclamation that the taking of this man's life constitutes the *ransom* of many. If the cross is inspiration alone, from what, we might ask, have we been set free? How have we been transformed, made ready and able for a life of obedience and *imitatio Christi*?

Atonement as a coherent doctrine appears to be on the horns: either it is objective, and therefore involved in an economy of exchange that deconstructs conceptually, or it is subjective, and God does not act through the cross except to inform and inspire. The reader will not be surprised to learn that from here we will offer up a third way. In the previous chapter we demonstrated that deploying maternal labor as a model for the cross helps us understand how the cross addresses sin: as the God-born, the spiritual children birthed at the cross possess a divine nature and the potential and propensity to live and act as God lives and acts. Moreover, as children embedded into the divine family that constitutes the church, the God-born are formed and nurtured in such a way as to bring this potential to its fruition. By all accounts, the cross as the labor of God generates an objective model of atonement in which real, God-authored change takes place in people. It is now our burden to show that, in addition, this model also avoids the conceptual deconstruction that besets traditional objective models like substitution, satisfaction, and victor/ransom.

A Conceptual Analysis of Objective Atonement, Exchange, and the Gift

In Christian theology the substitute, sacrifice, or ransom must be a gift. Goats have no choice in the matter; Christ ostensibly did. In the Incarnate Word and in his cruciform death, God graciously intercedes on behalf of the human race, gifting God's incarnate self to us for us. But what sort of "gift" is this? Since at least Friedrich Nietzsche's *Genealogy of Morals*, philosophers and theologians have complicated the notion of a gift, of giftedness.[6] Although aspects of Nietzsche's history are certainly overwrought, he rightly locates gifting within economies of exchange. That is, "gifts" fundamentally address social concerns of credit and debt. Nietzsche is ultimately both awed and horrified by "Christianity's stroke of genius: none other than God sacrificing himself for man's debt, none other than God paying himself back . . . the creditor sacrificing himself out of love . . . out of *love* for his debtor!"[7] Thinking anthropologically, Nietzsche argues that Christianity's idea is a method of human temporary self-medication. Its goal, in fact, is to escape—to free its adherents from an economy of exchange, to be freed from infinite and unpayable debt. Of course Nietzsche thinks that this is something human beings have created and foisted upon themselves, but the religious idea is meant to offer "a martyred humanity . . . temporary relief."[8] Temporary indeed, because once human beings have comprehended the magnitude of this "gift," they are immediately thrown into the cycle of credit and debt once again. Such magnanimity from God demands—what else?—infinite and unpayable gratitude and obedience. The solution perpetuates the problem.

Thinking along these lines then led Jacques Derrida to deconstruct the idea of giftedness entirely.[9] In order for a gift to remain a gift—that is, free—Derrida suggests that it must be fundamentally excised from any possibility of reciprocity. If reciprocity can result, the gift is not free, and another cycle of exchange has been elicited. To avoid reciprocity, the recipient must not recognize the gift as a gift at all, lest a desire to reciprocate arise. Simultaneously, the giver ought not to know her own gift as gift or she might receive self-gratification from having given, or, as Derrida puts it, the giver "gives back to himself symbolically the value of what he thinks he has given."[10] Therefore, thinks Derrida, the gift cannot appear to be a gift at all. If it is known as a gift, it will initiate again the cycle of exchange. Thus, there cannot be any actual gifts; the gift is a chimera, something thought but never experienced, for to experience it is to revoke its giftedness as such.[11]

Derrida's paradox should not be taken lightly. This is not because he has somehow put God in a bind—we should wonder from the outset if the God who expects obedience from liberated slaves is terribly concerned about human beings sensing that they are in debt. In fact, in Paul's disquisition in Romans 6, the apostle evinces a kind of reveling in a particular sort of servitude. The aorist participles in vv. 18 and 22 (ἐδουλώθητε, δουλωθέντες) are divine passives, indicating that God has done the "enslaving."[12] Derrida would no doubt find this appalling, as God has apparently been quite happy to allow the Roman Christians to go from laboring under one kind of debt to another. The obvious suggestion, then, is that "gift" or "giftedness" is a category mistake. Whatever has happened between God and human beings in and through Jesus Christ, calling it a "gift" is misleading in at least one important way: it frames the logic by which God acts in terms unsuitable to the nature of either God or God's gracious initiatives. There can be no doubt that human beings have received the incarnation and crucifixion in terms of economies of exchange. Derrida crucially exposes our language about gifts for what it is: misdirection. But the biblical witness goes further still, for God's nature and God's actions not only supersede but "explode" economies of exchange.[13]

Paul Ricoeur's exegesis of the "gift" (χάρισμα)[14] preached by the apostle Paul in Romans 5:6-21 is worth recounting at length:

> Thus the memorial is a transcended past, on which one can confer neither the status of illusion, from which one would be delivered, without relapse, by a simple movement of demythologization at the service of our thought, nor that of an eternal law of truth, which would find in the atonement of the Just One its supreme confirmation. Punishment is more than an idol to break and less than a law to idolize. It is an economy which "marks an epoch" and which preaching retains in its memory of the Gospel. If the wrath of God no longer had any meaning for me, I would no longer understand what pardon and grace signify; but if the logic of punishment had its own meaning, if it were sufficient unto itself, it would be forever invincible as a law of being; the atonement of Christ would have to be inscribed within this logic, and this would be the greatest victory, because it occurs in the theologies of "vicarious satisfaction," which remain theologies of punishment and not of gift and grace.[15]

The "transcended memorial" is the Torah, the law of God. Ricoeur is trying to explain how Paul understands the point of the law. The law is over and done with: the "logic of punishment" has been transcended, but not left behind in its entirety. That is, it occupies a strange cognitive ground: neither "idol to break" nor "eternal law of truth." To grant the law either of these statuses is not only to give it too much or too little accord: it is fundamentally to lose contact with "pardon and grace." As he says a bit earlier, "It is only when we have crossed the border, into grace, that we can look back on what we have been exempted from."[16] We might say that the language of law, punishment, gift, and grace is only of use for us, for human beings.[17] These concepts are a subjective, reflexive response to the enormity, the weight of God on a cross. To reckon it properly, to stand experientially before what God has done is to hold the concept of legal violation and deserved punishment in the offing, as it were, neither the dismissed, valueless idol nor the continuing economy of which we are a part. If the former, we cannot receive Christ as a gift of any sort (for from what have we been saved?). If the latter, then the cross is once again caught up and reduced to just another *human* episode of debt and credit. For this is exactly what we should fear most: that Christ could be "inscribed within this logic" where "this logic" is the life, the culture, the social relations of human beings and human beings only. If Christ's death can be accurately—and in content exhaustively—characterized as a "payment" or a "substitution" or a "sacrifice," then atonement theology is itself reduced to anthropomorphism. Nietzsche is right: human beings have constructed for themselves a god who can relieve them— for a while, at least—from their embeddedness within an economy of credit and debt. If we are to claim convincingly that Nietzsche is wrong, Ricoeur points the way: credit and debt must be transcended. What is wanted, then, is an account of Scripture that does justice to the language of giftedness while nevertheless testifying to a model of atonement that is not mired in an economy of exchange. In what follows, we build just such an account.

The content—if not the tropes—of Paul's argument in Romans 5 is a denunciation of the economy of exchange as such. Yes, Paul uses language drawn from his life and culture and so speaks of gifts, grace, and dominion; but, no, Paul does not use this language to reify an economy of exchange. He uses it to describe how God in Christ has transcended exchange entirely.

It is true that Paul's use of gift language in Romans 1–8 is in keeping with the Greco-Roman conventions articulated by Seneca and these conventions surely conform to an economy of exchange.[18] In a sense this should be noncontroversial. When Paul speaks about gifts and gift-giving, he draws on the cultural presuppositions within which he lives and breathes. So if the Greco-Roman world regards the ideal gift as (1) being an end in itself (and thus not requiring reciprocity), (2) directed toward a person with whom one has a personal relationship, and (3) part of a shared economy of harmonious relations, then we should not be surprised if these features are present in and through

Paul's description of God's gift to humanity in Christ. However, such an analysis is flawed not because it situates Paul within Paul's culture—one would be hard-pressed to suggest that Paul does not think in terms circumscribed by the culture(s) of which he is a part—but because it fails to reckon with the *Sache* of Paul's discourse. Paul is engaged in talk about God, and when one talks about God one takes advantage of the words at hand; nevertheless, one is also aware that these words must be ready to wobble and stretch as they struggle to find purchase on a reality they are not inherently equipped to grasp.

It is precisely this wobbling and stretching that metaphorical religious language is perfectly suited to enact.[19] Whatever we mean when we say "gift," we should not expect its purchase on the divine to leave it unchanged. That is, giftedness, if as a concept it truly describes something that has happened between God and human beings in and through the cross, will see its meaning altered in accordance with the weight of glory, as it were. It is to this alteration that we now turn, keeping our eyes fixed on the cross as the labor of God and the way in which this particular characterization might transcend exchange once and for all, liberating the gift of God from economies of exchange, and transforming our notion of giftedness as such.

The Cross as the Labor of God: Gift Transcending Exchange

Atonement theology has, therefore, made a tremendous category mistake. By applying a credit/debt notion of giftedness to the cross and invoking economies of exchange in order to explain what Jesus' death did, our objective atonement models commit two equally egregious sins. Firstly, they fail exegetically, treating Paul's language of the gift as though he were speaking of an exchange among friends and not the terrible majesty of a crucified God. This is not the place to investigate the etiology of such an error, though something of Barth's sense that only "theological exegesis" could rescue the church from the bloodless rule of Liberal Protestantism's endless criticism is surely close to the mark. Secondly, atonement theology's models have inscribed an eternal recurrence—to plunder Nietzsche's rhetoric—of debt into a transhistorical event that was meant to break indebtedness once and for all. Rather than picturing the cross as God giving humanity a gift—and here something like the narrative of *Christus Victor* comes much closer to the actuality of atonement than any objective atonement model—atonement theology must once again reckon the cross as sundering every chain. Theology itself must atone for both the exegetical and conceptual sins, and, as we will now argue, accomplishing the first sets the stage for acknowledging the cross as the labor of God as the key to the second.

N. T. Wright's translation of Romans 5:17 may help us begin rehearing the "gift" in all of Paul's theological profundity: "For if, by the trespass of the one, death reigned through that one, how much more will those who receive the abundance of grace, and of the gift of covenant membership, of 'being in the right,' reign in life through the one man Jesus the Messiah."[20] The translation is notable primarily for the gloss of τῆς δωρεᾶς τῆς δικαιοσύνης, where Wright has understood "the gift of righteousness" as "the gift of covenant membership," which is another way of saying "being in the right." The claim is essentially that to have the status labeled "righteous" is to be included within a particular kind of election, namely those with whom God has covenanted. And in this people, this community of the covenanted, "life" now reigns; a new kind of experience has been inaugurated. It is interesting that Wright, by reading the "righteousness of God" (δικαιοσύνη θεοῦ) as basically covenantal, follows Ricoeur's reading of Romans and particularly Romans 5. Ricoeur calls God's righteousness "hyperjuridical" because "the juridical conceptual system has never exhausted the meaning of the Covenant." The covenant "has never ceased to designate a living pact, a community of destiny, a bond with creation, which infinitely surpasses the relation of right."[21] Thus, the "gift" of Romans 5 is God's declaration that the "weak" (5:6), the "sinners" (5:8), and God's "enemies" (5:10) have all been made partners in the covenantal community. Those once far off have been brought near.

But to be in covenant with God has, for Paul, a particular meaning. It means being a part of the successful "rescue of the Adam-project,"[22] which is a robust notion of "salvation," that is, " 'rescue from sin'; where 'sin,' *hamartia*, is the deadly infection of the whole human race, Israel included."[23] The reader will note that we have returned to where we began in the previous chapter: God, in Christ at the cross, has remedied the widespread disorder of sin. Creation, individual hearts, infected systems—all that are part and parcel of the covenant community have been rescued, fixed, healed, from the inside out. This is the "free gift" of Romans 5. It is not, the reader will also notice, an exchange.

This is a critical point because it is precisely here that Paul recognizes the content of what God has done and struggles to name it. Rather than offer a substitutionary gift—one that will invoke yet another economy of exchange—God in Christ has created a new community—one remedied from the various disorders of sin, one that in its very nature has transcended exchange entirely.[24] God is not "granting justification" or "inspiring sanctification" so much as beginning the end of a world dominated by just these sorts of mundane, pedestrian, and wholly powers-owned economic practices. Rather than a pardon or a mercy—however extensive such pronouncements may be—the gift of the cross is better understood as a new creation, a cosmological event instantiated in what theologians call ecclesiology. A new people, the God-born, gathered in a new family, the church, established as a landmark, a monument, signifying to the economies of the powers that another economy entirely already rules in the highest heavens and will one day do so always and everywhere. This is the divine "gift," and it is unserved by atonement models that denigrate it, reducing it to the tit-for-tat of favors asked and granted and returned. This is, of course, why ecclesiology must be sourced in labor and atonement, in the notion that the church is, fundamentally, the *family* of God, sharing God's character and proclivities by birth, rather than as something extrinsic to nature.[25] The family inculcates and nurtures and reinforces a way of being-in-the-world that is mostly unrecognizable to the world, saturated as it is by what we may now deem the disease of reciprocity.

When seen as the labor of God, the cross is an instrument through which God produces objective change, but not by exchange. Jesus does not mount the cross so that we do not have to, or some similar pseudo-theological pabulum. Rather, Mother Jesus births us into the family into which all humanity truly and most fully belongs. The Christian born from the cross locates herself within the remedied covenant community—by birth. Birth is received not as a "gift" but as something into which one is simply thrown, immediately and unconsciously, for this is how human beings come to be children of God.[26] And should we be so inclined to answer Derrida's puzzle about the possibility of a true gift, it is in the encounter between Paul's gift language and the image of the cross as labor that the supposedly chimerical Derridean gift is found—because, of course, the labor of the cross is not literally labor at all; it is an execution. This mother does not know herself as "mother." She does not experience this death as "giving birth." Instead, Jesus suffers death, and it is through this that God ushers the second birth into the world. And thus it is that the second birth is not *known* as a gift at all, for, insofar as it is experienced simply as being a child of God, it is known as all experiences of self-consciousness within a family: immediate and unmediated. We say, "My father is so-and-so, and this is as it has always been and as it should be." Only within our second-order reflection on the nature of our covenantal relations do we perceive our *Sitz im Leben* as "gifted" in the self-deconstructing Derridean sense. Paul's use of gift language is the only available expression of what has come to pass in Christ: the end of human—that is, sinful, unremedied—economies (i.e. economies of exchange) entirely. Labor and birth, by conceiving of the cross outside of the language of exchange, do away with the problem of the gift by changing what "giftedness" is. When "for us" is known transactionally, the logic of exchange cannot fail to rear up and endanger atonement theology of deconstruction. When "for us" is known instead in the birthing pangs by which we are thrown into God's family, we have a model that maps more accurately onto the ontology of the divine action of the cross and the history as it is given in the Gospels. This, we now suggest, is why models built on substitution or sacrifice appear inchoate upon deeper analysis, and why Christian atonement theology features its own amalgamating logic, fusing the metaphorical logics of the images from whence it came: insofar as transaction forms the core of atonement, the problem of the gift remains.

To put it all another way, the logic of transaction deconstructs because the "gift" that is Christ must be absurd within any possible economy of exchange. And we have already noted this, though perhaps not in quite this fashion. The innocent girl hoping to be executed that the murderer might go free is absurd. But this is because, ultimately, the economy of exchange is itself fatally flawed, pointing beyond itself to an eschatological regime in which exchange is itself transcended. The idea of a little girl trying to take the place of a vicious criminal is tragicomically laughable, but only a bit more so than *anyone* taking the murderer's place. Murderers' places are not to be taken; taking a murderer's place does not ultimately solve the problem of a murderer having murdered. A life has been snuffed out. No substitution will bring the victim back. Exchange does not actually do anything constructive. Human sacrifice—and here we leave to the side Girard's sociological critique and take the practice at face value—suffers from the same fundamental absurdity: a substitute, a different sacrifice, a different victim is not what is needed. Sacrifice itself needs to end. Economies of exchange deconstruct insofar as they are incapable of doing what needs to be done. What is needed is for the machine of exchange itself to be sabotaged, and sabotaged in such a way as to eliminate the very problems the machine was invented to solve. In this case, namely, the problem is sin in all of its distorting, corrupting, ruining ignominy. If only there were something, some kind of gift-that-was-not-a-gift, a way out of exchange altogether, something that defenestrated sin and exposed it and transformed people from what they are into what they ought to be. As we gaze at the labor of God, birthing spiritual children out of the cycles of exchange, perhaps we can cry out with Paul in Romans 7:24-25 (NRSV), "Wretched man that I am! Who will rescue me from this body of death? Thanks be to God through Jesus Christ our Lord!"

Labor and Birth: Escaping the Cycles of Sin and Exchange

Transactional models of atonement have difficulty addressing two issues that are—as we have now seen—conceptually related. In the previous chapter we noted that atonement must address a biblically robust understanding of sin and show how the cross solves the problem of sin in all of its corrupting systems. Here we have reckoned with the problem that has faced all atonement models built on economies of exchange. Derrida's problem of the gift helps us understand why transactional notions of atonement end up with contorted internal logics, bizarre theological constructs given to absurdity. The fact of the former ultimately dooms the latter, for no exchange can put sin to rights. But where transactional models falter, the labor and birth model persists. Something creative, something unprecedented has happened at the cross, something that has made human beings true children of God, sharing in their Father's character as befits those who share blood. In Romans 5, Paul calls this newness a gift, but in so doing he annihilates the economy of exchange that gifts and giftedness imply, replacing it with the covenantal family, the family that—thanks to the labor of the cross—the weak, the sinners, and the enemies of God can claim as their birthright.

6

EXPANDING THE AGONY OF THE CROSS
How Labor Opens Fresh Theological Frontiers

We have argued at length that spent metaphors, repetition, and misapplied categories have robbed the proclamation of the cross of its hideous splendor and therefore of much of its power. But it is not only the various traditional concerns of atonement—say, the way the cross addresses humanity's sin problem—that have worn thin and withered. The present chapter argues that a strong reorientation to the cross as the labor of God will enliven other domains as well, offering fresh entry points into classical doctrines like election and pneumatology. This should come as no surprise; we have seen already how the labor of God impinges on doctrines of creation, ecclesiology, and impassibility, among others. These doctrines had to be revisited in light of the cross itself imaged as God's childbirth; we now have the opportunity to hold out the labor of God like a torch, allowing its insights into the nature of the Godhead to reorient and refigure and hopefully renew everything from our understanding of God's election of Israel, to the soteriological and eschatological work of the Spirit, to the divine processions of the immanent Trinity. The goal is not to be exhaustive but to demonstrate the lasting theological currency of the labor of God. To put it differently, if theology resembles an interweaving of beliefs, then we may expect a radical reconfiguration of atonement to dramatically shift the woof and warp of the whole tapestry. So it is that creation is much closer to atonement in light of labor. And ecclesiology is derived from travail. Let us now look further out to begin to see how the ripples of travail alter other domains.

Election as Travail: How Choosing Israel Hurts

What has the election of Israel to do with the cross? Biblical theology sometimes tries to begin to answer this question by appealing to the grand narrative of Scripture, suggesting that Jesus takes up the mission of representing Israel's holy vocation rightly, exercising dominion over the powers and conforming ideally to the logics of the law and the prophets. In this, Jesus is superior to Moses, who was himself an embodiment of Israel-as-chosen-of-Yahweh.[1] Like many prophets, Jesus' commitment to God's message and rule seals his fate and destines him for an ignominious death. And this makes good narratival sense. Israel needs a representative to fulfill its vocation; Jesus takes up this mantle and, subsequently, the cross as well. Israel is chosen to be a holy people; Jesus accomplishes this divine election on its behalf.

Whatever we make of this left-to-right reading of the Old and New Testaments, theology must be left dissatisfied. Who is the electing God? What is God's election like? On what basis does it take place? Even if the story of Jesus-as-Israel is true in all the particulars, it only raises the profile of these deeper questions. With a doctrine of divine labor, however, we are poised to offer an account of Israel's election that is cross shaped, in which Israel's election itself—and really every instance of divine election—is a divine act of birth accompanied by travail. In what follows, we will see how a theologically and textually sensitive construal of Moses' Song in Deuteronomy 32, in which the relations between God and Israel are imaged as the relations holding between parent(s) and child, construes election as a particular kind of labor pain.

The Song of Moses: God the Faithful Mother/Father

Deuteronomy 32:1-43, the "Song of Moses," has been the subject of intense scholarly scrutiny. Among the standard points of interest, date of composition, structural analysis, text criticism, and intertextual relationships with Deutero-Isaiah dominate the landscape.[2] This can in some ways skew the theological picture that arises from more literary concerns.[3] The two principal images the poet uses for God are the Rock and the Parent.[4] In 32:18, these two images are united, the poet reminding Israel, "You were unmindful of the Rock that bore you; you forgot the God who gave you birth." The first verb relating to birth, *yld*, can refer both to the mother's act of giving birth (e.g., Genesis 3:16) or to the father's act of begetting (e.g., Proverbs 23:22). The second, however, *hûl*, exclusively refers to the mother's birthing process. In Deuteronomy 32:18, the verb is in the polel—just as in Psalm 90:2[5]—and conjures images of labor and the pain associated with it. It is likely that God is being imaged as both father and mother, a sort of complete divine parent. In effect, 32:18 sums up the descriptions of God's character in the first two sections of the song (vv. 1-15, 16-29),[6] and it fuses the associations we have with God-as-Rock and God-as-Parent. This is worth noting because it frees us from deciding which aspects of God's relationship to Israel are associated with God-as-Rock, which are to be understood as God-as-Father, and which are God's motherly propensities. The textual joining displays its deeper theological truth: the Lord is One, and no characteristic of the God-Israel relationship can or should be reduced to being "rock-like," "fatherly," or "motherly." Instead, we should let each of the descriptors counter our intuitions about what rocks or fathers or mothers are like.

God is perfect, just, faithful, and true (v. 5). God's child Israel, however, is corrupt, ruined, and deceitful (v. 6). The Lord guarded, protected, shielded, and provided in wilderness deserts (v. 10). Like a mother eagle God sheltered Israel in the nest and taught him to fly by letting the young bird alight on her pinions (v. 11).[7] God feeds and nurses[8] Israel with the fruits of the land (vv. 13-14), but in the end the son grows up to be bloated and spoiled, consorting with foreign gods, forgetting the Rock-Father-Mother that bore and faithfully raised him (vv. 16-18). This behavior enrages God, who decides to judge his children, but not to extinction (vv. 19-35). At the right time, the Lord's anger will relent and will pour out compassion on the people (vv. 36-43).

The mothering God undergoes the pain of labor in anticipation of a lifelong commitment to her offspring. As parent, God's perfect, faithful character issues in a consummate performance of all standard parenting tropes: provision, protection, and training.[9] Like the unconditionally loving father or mother, God remains committed to Israel even after his terrible rebellion. God's vindication of the son even clears God's own reputation as a good and faithful parent in the eyes of the nations (vv. 26-27).

Moses offers his song, however, as a warning and a comfort. In chapter 31, he gives as a reason for the poem the fact that he knows he is about to die and that, without his leadership, Israel will be even more rebellious than it was while Moses yet lived (31:29). The context of the entire poem is an expectation of future failure. God labors to bring this son to birth with a full expectation that the pain of parenthood is going to last long after the birthing travails. In fact, from the divine perspective, the pain of rebellion and loss is surely incorporated into the election of Israel itself. That is, part of God's election of Israel is labor pain, the pain of bringing Israel into being and the anticipatory pain of knowing that such labors will end in frustration and loss of the son and the pain of the various rescues God will undertake to win him back. In terms of the divine economy, then, the election of Israel is cross shaped, cruciform. Or to approach it from the point of view of the question that began this section, the cross is more than the logical conclusion of, say, Jesus bearing Israel's vocation on its behalf; it is instead in keeping with the shape and character of God's electing Israel itself. What it is for God to choose a special people is for God to embrace travail. The cross expresses in incarnate manifestation what it was for the Mothering God of Moses' Song to bear Israel, her son.

Election hurts. And, surprisingly, it is labor pain itself that connects election and cross: God's commitment to Israel hurt, and it reaches its most excruciating travail when God expands the election of Israel to include the nations. This widening is, as we have argued extensively, the labor of the cross, where Mother Jesus births spiritual children. And by including election with creation and atonement as instances of divine labor, we are implicitly arguing for a further dynamic in the divine economy, the issuing of the life-giving, renewing, regenerating Spirit through the Son's travails. It is to this pneumatological implication that we now turn.

Death and Life, Son and Spirit

The apostle Paul famously tells the Corinthian church that "if anyone is in Christ, there is new creation" (2 Corinthians 5:17). The NRSV smooths in English what in Greek is abrupt and revelatory, adding "there is" where Paul offers no copula (εἴ τις ἐν Χριστῷ, καινὴ κτίσις). Paul understands the Spirit as having a twofold nature: weakness and power, or "power and cruciformity."[10] To be "in Christ" is to be participating in his crucifixion by the Spirit. That is, the Spirit "links Paul to the cross, and via the cross to Christ in suffering and to others in love."[11] As such, the Spirit has "an active killing function."[12] So the Spirit mediates our death in accordance with Christ's own death. The Spirit's "killing function," however, is not without purpose. It enables the Spirit's primary, vivifying ministry. For now, "the Spirit powerfully brings life out of sin and death; in the future, the same Spirit will give life to the dead in parallel to the raising of Jesus. In other words, the Spirit is life because the Spirit *transforms* death into life."[13] This is how we make sense of Paul's "in Christ"/"new creation" dynamic. The Spirit unites us to Christ in death so that the natural consequence of divine death—that is, new life by the Spirit—may be ours as well. Applying the metaphor of childbirth to Jesus' death on the cross illuminates a Trinitarian dynamic at work: the Word labors unto death, the Spirit issues forth in new life. Out of Jesus' mothering death comes new vivifying life according to the nature and work of the third hypostasis. At the cross, therefore, the Spirit proceeds through the Son's travail.

In Romans 8 Paul sounds these same notes, but in a context that will lead to the renewal of creation (the first labor of God) and, in chapters 9–11, Israel's election—God's second economic travail. He begins by thinking through the implications of Jesus' resurrection. Jesus does not remain dead; no, he is raised in the Spirit (8:11). Since this is the case, and since it is the case that Christians have this same Spirit, we may look forward to a similar future. A bit further on, Paul recognizes the same dynamic at work in the creation as a whole. It was subjected to futility, yes, but this cannot last. The same transformation from decay that our bodies will have by the Spirit will be known when the created order's birth pangs too come to an end. God's self-abnegation in the Son through whom the created order comes into being has its final result in the Spirit bringing fresh life out of decay. In a sense, the whole cosmos imitates the labor of God on the cross and therefore expects the same birth-to-life that always follows divine travail. This logic gives Paul hope as he goes on to Romans 9–11, where he expresses his conviction that Israel will not remain far off. Commenting on the section as a whole, N. T. Wright observes the following:

> The hope remained the Jewish hope: the resurrection of the dead, as the centerpiece of the renewal of all creation, the flooding of God's world with justice and joy. It was transformed

by the belief that this had already happened in and through
Jesus, and in and through those in whom the spirit now dwelt,
and that the still-future aspects of this hope would happen by
exactly the same means. And that meant, of course, that hope
was confirmed as such: "Hope in turn," wrote Paul, "does not
make us ashamed, because the love of God has been poured out
in our hearts through the holy spirit who has been given to us"
(Romans 5:5).[14]

Romans 9–11 cannot be sundered from 5–8 because Paul is
reconfiguring—among other things—his understanding of election
around the arrival of "Jesus and the spirit." Jesus' Spirit-empowered
resurrection and the transforming life of the Spirit have made the
unthinkable possible: the inclusion of the gentiles into the people of
God. And it is the radicality of the invasion of the Spirit that gives Paul
the conviction that even though not all ethnic Jews recognize Jesus
as Messiah, the end is nevertheless clear. The same God who initi-
ates life in the Spirit through the career of Jesus cannot possibly allow
Israel to remain far off. These are God's people; they who have been
laboriously elected cannot simply wallow in decay and frustration. The
death of the Word leads to life in the Spirit; the dynamics of Romans
5–8 do not simply cease to operate; Paul must incorporate them into
his theology of Israel's election. Israel is God's creation, brought about
by the electing Word—the electing Word who anticipates from the
beginning Israel's rebellion—and so Israel too must benefit from the
death-into-life-in-the-Spirit dynamic. This is just how God works, so
we can anticipate new life and new hope among the people of Israel
just as we may anticipate the same for our own decaying bodies and
the cosmos that has until now endured frustration and futility. In each
case the Word's self-abnegating creation, election, and atonement are
followed by the procession of the Spirit into the gift of new life.

What we know of God's atoning election at the cross may be pos-
ited of God's election always and everywhere such that even God's
birth of Israel includes the painful being-for constitutive of the
Word's anticipation of Israel's frustrating rebellion. Note the symme-
try between the Son's anticipation of flesh and crucifixion and God's
anticipation of Israel's waywardness. The frustration, the labor, is there
from the beginning. But it is not just labor. God's labor anticipates successful birth—that is, new life—and specifically new life in the Spirit.

Creation will not forever be subjected to futility, Israel will not forever wander away from God, and Jesus will not just stay dead. Rather, in each case the Word's self-abnegation leads to—nay, produces—new life by the Spirit. Reconceiving of creation, election, and the cross in terms of birthing travail attunes theology to symmetries that ground— or, to borrow from German theology, provide the *Urstruktur* of—the divine economy itself. The labor-of-God/birth-in-the-Spirit dynamic is like a divine fingerprint: wherever God is at work, we should expect to see labor and birth.

For this reason, it is worth demonstrating that this dynamic, this fingerprint, is not merely consigned to historical or cosmic acts, what an older argot might have named interventions. That is, the same God who released creation, election, and atonement from labor in the past unleashes the Spirit in Christian soteriological *experience* in the present. And it is just this kind of redescription of Christian life that we find in 1 Peter when the author reflects on our new birth through the Word.[15]

New Birth through the Word in 1 Peter

In the logic of 1 Peter, new birth occurs in our present lives in an act of God in which the Spirit issues through the Son's labor to bring new life. The dynamics we have already noted in Israel's birth, creation's cosmic rebirth, and Paul's convictions about the future redemption of Jews who do not yet recognize the Messiah are recapitulated even in the experience of new birth in the present day. The Word labors; the Spirit proceeds through the Word to bring new life. To make this case, we will review the logic of the letter as a whole, contextualizing its ethical commands as operating out of a theologically reconfigured sense of time. Within this broader picture, in which the death and resurrection of Jesus stand as both the inauguration of the End and a fixed point in the past that is accessed by spiritual revelation in the present, the Christian receives life in the Spirit through existential awareness of the Son's death and resurrection.[16] Thus it is that the present experience of salvation, in which the Spirit brings the good news of Christ's suffering and glory, is the existential manifestation of the event of cross and resurrection. Just as it is through Christ on the cross that the Spirit brings resurrection life at a point in history, so it is through the message of the cross that the Spirit enlivens human beings in the present.[17]

As the author of 1 Peter puts it, new birth comes "through the word of God." The message is about Jesus; it is brought in life-giving power by the Spirit. Or, as we have already suggested, the Spirit proceeds to us through the Word.

In 1 Peter 1:3-4, God's great mercy has issued in a "new birth" (ἀναγεννήσας) in which there is an "inheritance that is imperishable, undefiled, and unfading." In context, it becomes clear that though the terminology is a bit slippery, "new birth," "inheritance," and, variously, "living hope" (1:3) and "glorious joy" (1:8) all refer to salvation.[18] We might be tempted to think, then, that new birth is something exclusively reserved for God's future rescue; this would be a mistake. In 1 Peter, the new birth has already taken place. The aorist participle ἀναγεννήσας ("the Begetter")[19] sets God's birthing action as antecedent to the present state of Peter's audience. This strongly suggests— and Peter's later language concerning the timing and purpose of his audience's suffering confirms—that new birth has indeed already come to the letter's recipients. Nevertheless, the newborn inheritors of God's manifold mercy, though born into their eschatological inheritance, have not yet received it in full. They are effectively standing with a foot planted firmly in each of two worlds: the first, the time of their present suffering, is subject to the normal standards of space and time; the second, God's eschatological salvation, reaches back from the end with all the weight of eternity, impressing on his new children the purpose and transience of their present status.[20]

The textual soil here is theologically rich, featuring several explicit references to the Old Testament (1:16, 24), considerations about the nature of prophecy (vv. 10-12), and what has come to be thought of in systematic theology as election (1:2, 20). Cutting a swathe through this dense theological thicket is at once both daunting and artificial. How can we relate these weighty themes to Peter's concept of new birth, and how can we avoid placing undue emphasis on what appears to be a subsidiary element of the discourse as a whole?

The answer depends on retaining focus on Peter's overarching aim, a diasporic ecclesial ethic.[21] When we pass from the letter's preliminary considerations to its heart, we find, for example, Peter mining the Suffering Servant of Isaiah 53 to offer succor, encouragement, and a theological explanation for present suffering of Christian slaves (2:19-25). A bit earlier Peter enjoins readers to resist the use of freedom for evil (2:16) and to accept pagan authorities "for the Lord's sake" (2:13). These sorts of maddening ethical injunctions abound throughout the letter. With respect to earthly authorities, Peter's logic assumes the ultimate illegitimacy of human institutions (and, one might think, rightly so given their treatment of the Lord whom Christians confess). Nevertheless, readers are to do right in the eyes of provincial governors so as to earn their praise and silence critics (2:13-15). Christians thus curry favor from inauthentic rulers and are called to give them the very honor denied both to Christ and to themselves. Christian wives of pagan husbands are commanded to act as if these husbands have genuine authority when—like emperors, provincial governors, and slave owners—they obviously do not (3:1-2). In point of fact, the simile "as if" defines a great deal of Peter's ethical discourse. There is an actual reality of which Christians are aware. In this real world, they are "a chosen race, a royal priesthood, a holy nation, God's own people" (2:9 NRSV), and yet they must act as if the humiliating social order that alienates and others them operates legitimately.[22] Even setting aside the questionable utility of this strategy for evangelism and averting further social ostracism, we must be taken aback at the audacity of Peter's assumptions. What sort of people could reasonably be expected to act like this?

Just putting the question this way is, of course, to have ignored or radically misunderstood the letter's first section, where the primary question Peter addresses is one of identity.[23] The rhetorical push should not be missed. We, the readers Peter addresses, are "exiles of the dispersion" (1:1) and "suffer[ing] various trials" (1:6). This experienced reality is relativized, however, by who we are. We are the "chosen and destined by God" (1:2), those who have a "living hope" and an "imperishable inheritance" (1:3-4). We are "protected by the power of God" to "salvation," a salvation into which the prophets themselves "inquired carefully" (vv. 5, 9, 10-11). The radical disjunction between our experienced reality and the cosmic truth about our identity only makes sense when we theologically reconceive of time itself.[24] Green's account of time in the above-cited article "Narrating the Gospel in 1 and 2 Peter" demonstrates how the story Peter tells the community about itself has cognitive effects. Human identity is composed out of narrative; Peter's narrative explains who we really are, why we are not experiencing what we expect, and how these experiences relate to our ultimate end. The otherwise maddening ethical commands make sense because they are aimed at forming us into certain kinds of people headed for a certain kind of end. As it happens, this end is an inheritance that is imperishable, undefiled, and unfading, kept in heaven (1:4).

Thus, the labor of God does not replace or nullify the real human experience of time and death. Instead, new birth irrevocably juxtaposes this experience with the eschatological inheritance of total salvation (1 Peter 1:4, 9),[25] and acknowledges a simultaneous experience of revivification in the Spirit. As persons now expecting to last, as those now participating in God's time, Peter's claim that various trials linger "for a little while" (v. 6) is not denigrating the lived experience of his readers; it is an understatement. Divine life, accessible to the born-anew by the Spirit, does not just relativize present suffering—it does so to the vanishing point.[26] What is honor paid to a false authority in the light of eschatological glory? Nothing, a blip, it is the grass that is scorched by nightfall. And what sort of person can live in this reality now? The one whose spiritual rebirth issues in "rejoicing" and "indescribable joy" (1:8). The emphasis on time is critical to getting a sense of new birth's importance in 1 Peter. New birth offers Christians in trying social circumstances "a living hope" (1:3) because they have been born through an "imperishable seed" (σπορᾶς ἀφθάρτου) that is "the living and enduring word of God" (διὰ λόγου ζῶντος θεοῦ καὶ μένοντος, 1:23).

On this reading of new birth through the word in 1 Peter, it becomes clear why the author expects such a radical ethic. It is not enough to suggest that God's message lingers in the minds of the Christian diaspora; instead, something altogether more essential is going on. The new birth juxtaposes the present experiences of the community with eschatological inheritance. And this is true insofar as it goes, but it fails to account for the real effects of the undying, imperishable seed of Christ. When sown in the ground, this seed does not face decay because the irrepressible, enlivening Spirit proceeds through it. The epistle of 1 Peter makes this explicit in 3:18b: "He was put to death in the flesh, but made alive in the Spirit." Likewise, the communities of faith addressed in 1 Peter continue to experience the Spirit's quickening, because they too were sown with Christ and they too, united with the imperishable seed, cannot but be the recipients of new life in the Spirit. The seed/word endures with them; it remains in them. In

1 Peter new birth means Spirit-mediated resurrection life—both now and in the eschaton—that proceeds through the imperishable seed that is the Word.[27] In Christian theology, this Word is the Son, the second hypostasis of the triune God.

Thus, present Christian experience of salvation and the eschatological consummation of which it is a prolepsis are further instances of a Trinitarian dynamic in the divine economy: the labor of the Word issues forth in new life in the Spirit. It is striking that the divine economy so consistently manifests in this way across the Scriptures, history, and now present and future soteriological experience. In fact, in conjunction with Rahner's dictum that the economic Trinity is the immanent Trinity, the labor of God that issues in new life in the Spirit gives us grounds for reasoning trinitarianly about, of all things, the filioque clause and the divine processions.

Moltmann on the Filioque

Few Western Christians have as loudly or as boldly called for excising the filioque clause from the Nicene Creed as Jürgen Moltmann, for whom it is "superfluous."[28] This is not to say that it is theologically incorrect—for reasons we shall examine momentarily—but the lasting schism between East and West must be eclipsed by Christian unity, and so, for Moltmann, the filioque clause ought to be removed. For Moltmann, and really for many in the Roman Catholic and Protestant worlds, the filioque clause secures the notion that "the Word, the Son, has a share in the production of the Holy Spirit, which cannot be reduced to the economic order."[29] The concern has always been that "the Son was 'not unrelated' to the Father in the production of the Spirit."[30] Moltmann claims, however, that whatever relations must be secured have been so by the fact that the Father is named Father and it is as Father that the Father produces the Spirit. For so long as he is known as Father, the Father's fatherhood is implicated and thus the Son's sonship. Thus, the Spirit, proceeding from the Father of the Son, is indirectly related to the Son regardless of whether or not the filioque clause remains in the creed. Since this is the case, Moltmann thinks, and since the clause has been the source of nigh endless controversy, it is in the best interests of all involved simply to drop it and let the subsequent and necessary "common discussion about the Doctrine of the Trinity" begin, since "the one is impossible without the other."[31]

The question of the inclusion of the filioque necessarily falls out of one's answer to a prior question, namely, does the Spirit always proceed from the Son in the divine economy? If so, then one supposes that Rahner's dictum holds and the filioque clause rightly characterizes the relations holding within the immanent Trinity. It would seem, of course, that in the incarnation itself, "the birth of the Son is so intensely accompanied by the procession of the Spirit from the Father that we have to say: the Son is begotten by the Father through the Spirit." This is likely a Trinitarian reading of the phrase πνεῦμα ἅγιον ἐπελεύσεται ἐπὶ σέ in Luke 1:35. Moreover, when Moltmann then suggests that, since the Spirit "accompanies" the birth of the Son, the Spirit therefore "*rests in the Son*,"[32] we are probably not far wrong to think that Moltmann is hearing John the Baptizer's testimony, that "the Spirit descended like a dove and rested on him" (ἔμεινεν ἐπ᾽ αὐτόν, John 1:32). Therefore, Moltmann thinks, since we have a "Spirit-history of Christ" in which the Spirit accompanies and dwells, rests, and/or indwells the Son, it is misleading at best to enshrine the Spirit's procession from the Father and "also from the Son" in the Nicene Creed.

Insofar as he goes, Moltmann is right in his emphasis on the Son and Spirit as both receiving their hypostasis from the Father's generation; he is also right to emphasize the Spirit's eternal comprehension of the Father as the Father of the Son. But this comprehension leads to more than the dictum that "the Father is never without the Son and nowhere acts without him, just as he is never without, and never acts without, the Spirit."[33] Moltmann is in danger of leaving the relations between Son and Spirit less than clearly defined. In creation, in election, at the cross, in soteriological experience and eschatological expectation, the Word labors to bring forth birth in the Spirit. Scripture's witness to the decisive actions of God across history and human hearts is uniform: the Spirit processes through the Son's labor at the cross, in the election and ultimate salvation of Israel, in cosmic redemption, and in our experience of new birth. We are on firm ground when we absolutely insist on something more than simply excising the filioque altogether. Moltmann's ecumenical instincts are admirable, but his argumentation cannot stand in light of revelation. Always and everywhere, the divine economy operates in a particular manner: the Son labors and the Spirit proceeds through the Son's labor, to bring new life. Theology must preserve this intra-Trinitarian dynamic.

Rethinking the Filioque: Procession "through the Son"

The logic of new birth follows Mother Jesus' death in childbirth with new life in the Spirit. This is the experience of the church, yes, but it is predicated on the work of the Godhead in the divine economy. If indeed the economic Trinity is the immanent Trinity, then it is therefore the case that the Spirit's vivifying nature processes from the Father through the Son such that the livelihood of the Godhead eternally flows through the Son. This is so because in his causation from the Father, the Spirit "comprehends" the Father as the Father of the Son, and thus the Father as the Father of the one-to-be-incarnate, the one-to-be-crucified, the one-to-be-mother-in-travail. To put it in Barthian terms, the Word is comprehended as Jesus Christ from eternity.[34] And thus from eternity the Spirit is the vivifier, the ever-quickener because the Spirit flows from eternity through the one-to-travail, the one-to-be-crucified. Economically, the Spirit transforms Jesus' death into life, the violence of the cross into the enlivening suffering of a mother. He is the one who raises to life, who reaps what the Son sows—it is the Son himself who is sown. This gives immanent language to the church's experience of the economic Trinity, in which the Spirit is known as the Spirit of the Son. It is the economic expression of the immanent flowing of the Spirit from the Father through the Son. In the divine economy, therefore, there is a reason that the Spirit brings forth life from death, bestows fresh flames on dying embers, and so forth. It is in the eternal nature of the Spirit to be the Spirit who flows through the Son, the from-eternity-Jesus-Christ.

Knowing the divine economy through the lens of the labor of God gives theology an image and a dynamic that has powerful implications for how the immanent Trinity is to be described. Since the Spirit's vivification—from eternity—proceeds from the Father through the Son and is paradigmatically expressed economically in the death and resurrection of Jesus the Messiah, and since this dynamic is preserved and expanded in the doctrines of creation, election, and soteriological and eschatological experience, then a truly ecumenical creed should enshrine this Trinitarian feature in its confession. Given the labor of God, theology can clarify the relationship between the Son and the Spirit by replacing "also from the Son" with "through the Son." "Through the Son" is suitable because it describes both the immanent flowing of the Spirit through the Son and the revealed divine economy in which the water and the blood pour out from the Son's side. The creedal formulation through the Son rightly unites the immanent and the economic and simultaneously protects the Father's monarchy. What is more, a designation such as through the Son is fully in keeping with the Trinitarian theology of Maximus the Confessor, who, reading the filioque as meaning that the Spirit proceeds "through the Son," offers "a solution to the problem—a solution that centuries later remains our best hope of resolving this troublesome ecumenical issue."[35] Even more encouragingly, Moltmann's own formulation, in which the Spirit is said to comprehend the Father's Fatherhood as Father of the Son in his procession, is drawn from, among others, Gregory of Nyssa and Maximus the Confessor.[36] In light of all this, perhaps the Eastern and Western churches could agree on a formulation more in keeping with the logic of Scripture, less historically fraught, and irenic in nature. To know the Spirit as coming διὰ τοῦ Υἱοῦ is to know the mothering and dying Word giving birth to eternal life in the Spirit. Just as the Scriptures testify that the Word of the Lord gives life, so too do we know this life in the enlivening of the church by the Spirit, and in the spilling of water and blood from Mother Jesus at the cross.

Labor of God: The Agony of the Cross and the Birth of the Spirit

We began our inquiry in the hope that rediscovering an image of the cross from the Scriptures and the tradition might breathe new life into the church's proclamation of the gospel and the "at-one-ment" of God and human beings and people with each other. The present chapter reorients that hope by undermining it entirely. For what we find is that even those designs are too parochial, too quotidian. Rather, the image found in the Fourth Gospel, in Anselm and Julian and Marguerite and Clement, has profound implications across theological domains. We have seen how the cross as labor transforms, for example, election as a painful prefiguration of atonement. We have seen how it re-recognizes the Holy Spirit as proceeding through the Son's self-abnegation to bring renewal and new life. And we have considered how present Christian soteriological experience and eschatological expectation too are illuminated by the labor of God.

Happily, however, this does not exhaust the matter. Indeed, fresh domains of inquiry nearly suggest themselves. What, in practical theology, might be made of the erstwhile evangelical proclamation of the gospel in which individuals must be "born again" to be saved? One wonders if that formulation might be taken much more seriously and perhaps expanded or filled out within a robust theology of the labor of God. Or what of feminist theology? As it addresses gender issues, it is worth wondering whether and how the male Jesus' motherhood might be a conceptual resource. Likewise, one wonders if theological anthropology might be afforded helpful theological touchstones when accounting for trans and intersexed communities.

The cross is, of course, Christianity's most recognizable symbol, and for good reason, since every telling of the gospel must feature the cross at its center. A fresh reckoning of the cross cannot fail to send ripples—or perhaps waves—throughout Christianity's construal of God, the universe, and human beings. The cross should not and must not and indeed cannot be hermetically sealed away from theology or, worse, taken up and tinkered with and examined and returned without a whisper as if nothing had happened at all. Instead, everything— violence, sin, the church, Israel, election, eschaton, and creed—must come under the clarifying and convicting and commissioning light afforded by the travail Jesus endured for the generation and sake of the God-born. This brief inquiry is but a start.

We began in the hope that recovering and taking seriously a faithful metaphor for the cross would give its proclamation new life and radicality. Implicated in that hope was a concordant suspicion: that granting the cross as the labor of God conceptual space to flourish might generate fresh ways of thinking about the doctrine of atonement and, perhaps, related theological domains. Those hopes have not, as the proverb worries, been deferred. Rather, the cross-as-travail, the long-ignored theological root, has, like desire fulfilled, grounded a tree of life, with robust theological branches that now stretch out. It is now for the church only to seize the labor of God and internalize its glorious depiction of the agony of the cross and the birth of the church. So fortified, we may expect the church to become radical again. Radical in her declaration of who God is, what God has done, and who we the God-born are and are called to be, for the life Mother Jesus has birthed in the Spirit, like the life of the Father, cannot be extinguished or overcome.

NOTES

1: Retrieving the Forgotten Root

1 Beverly Roberts Gaventa, *From Darkness to Light: Aspects of Conversion in the New Testament* (Minneapolis: Fortress, 1986), 130.

2 Gaventa, *From Darkness to Light*, 136–38.

3 William Orr and William Guy, *Living Hope: A Study of the New Testament Theme of Birth from Above* (Santa Fe, N.M.: Sunstone Press, 1989), 9.

4 J. Ramsey Michaels makes a similar point in his note on John 3:3, 7 (*John* [Grand Rapids: Baker, 1984]), as does Leon Morris (*The Gospel According to John* [Grand Rapids: Eerdmans, 1995], 188–89). Michaels is more oblique in his recent work (*The Gospel of John* [Grand Rapids: Eerdmans, 2010], 180), using "rebirth" and "from above."

5 Charles Talbert (*Reading John: A Literary and Theological Commentary on the Fourth Gospel and the Johannine Epistles* [New York: Crossroad, 1992], 98–99) points us to William Greese ("'Unless One Is Born Again': The Use of a Heavenly Journey in John 3," *JBL* 107 [1988]: 677–93) to explain Second Temple backgrounds concerning heavenly descent-ascent. When a character goes up to heaven, literary convention signals deification. Talbert cites tractate 13 of the gnostic *Corpus Hermeticum*, where a disciple of Hermes, Tat, must be reborn, i.e., "go up" to heaven, to achieve divine essence. Talbert wants to argue that something analogous is going on in John. The difference, of course, is that Jesus descends and ascends for us. Nicodemus does not need to go above to see the kingdom; he must receive the Spirit from above to do so (Talbert, *Reading John*, 101).

6 Gaventa (*From Darkness to Light*, 133–34) is right to refer to the ambiguity in ὕδωρ ζῶν in John 4:10-11. The woman at the well hears "running water" when Jesus is talking about "living water." John's audience, attuned to the

105

theological importance of "life," quickly decodes what must be spelled out inside the narrative.

7   I am by no means convinced that "receiving the Spirit" is entirely non-metaphorical or, as some theologians are fond of saying these days, "onto-theological."

8   Michaels, *Gospel of John*, 1001.

9   Michaels, *Gospel of John*, 1002. Cf. Teresa Okure, "The Significance Today of Jesus's Commission to Mary Magdalene," *IRM* 81 (1992): 177–88 (182).

10   Okure, "Jesus's Commission," 183.

11   Mark W. G. Stibbe, *John* (Sheffield: JSOT Press, 1993), 175.

12   See Caroline Walker Bynum's review in *Jesus as Mother: Studies in the Spirituality of the High Middle Ages* (Berkeley: University of California Press, 1982), especially ch. 4.

13   Anselm, *Prayers and Meditations of St. Anselm with the Proslogion* (trans. Benedicta Ward; New York: Penguin, 1973), 153.

14   Julian of Norwich, *Showings* (ed. and trans. Edmund Colledge and James Walsh; Mahwah, N.J.: Paulist, 1978), 298.

15   Marguerite D'Oingt, *The Writings of Margaret of Oingt, Medieval Prioress and Mystic (d. 1310)* (ed. and trans. Renate Blumenfeld-Kosinski; Newburyport, Mass.: Focus Information Group, 1990), 31.

16   See, e.g., Elizabeth A. Johnson, *She Who Is: The Mystery of God in Feminist Theological Discourse* (New York: Crossroad, 1994); cf. Murray Rae, "The Travail of God," *IJST* 5 (2003): 47–61 (51–52).

17   See Caroline Walker Bynum, *Fragmentation and Redemption: Essays on Gender and the Human Body in Medieval Religion* (New York: Zone Books, 1991), 99. The image is juxtaposed with a scene of Adam "giving birth" to Eve from his side. See also this book's cover artwork: drawn from a contemporaneous Moralized Bible with French (rather than Latin) text, it too features the juxtaposition of Eve being "born" from Adam's side and the church being born from the side of the crucified Christ (*Bible moralisée: Codex Vindobonensis 2554*).

18   Clement, *Paedagogos*, I.4, 6.

19   Rae, "Travail of God," 52.

20   Patricia Wilson-Kastner, *Faith, Feminism, and the Christ* (Philadelphia: Fortress, 1983), 104.

21   Rebecca D. Pentz, "Can Jesus Save Women?" in *Encountering Jesus: A Debate on Christology* (ed. Stephen T. Davis; Atlanta: John Knox, 1988), 77–110. We will recapitulate some of Pentz' work in chapter 5 below.

22   Colleen Carpenter Cullinan, "In Pain and Sorrow: Childbirth, Incarnation, and the Suffering of Women," *Cross Currents* 58 (2008): 95–107.

23   Mary Streufert, "Maternal Sacrifice as a Hermeneutics of the Cross," in *Cross Examinations: Readings on the Meaning of the Cross Today* (ed. Merit Trelstad; Minneapolis: Augsburg Fortress, 2006), 63–75.

24 Tania Oldenhage, "Jesus' Labor Pain: Rereading Birth and Crisis in the Passion Narratives," *Lectio Difficilior* 2 (2012), available online at http://www.lectio.unibe.ch/12_2/oldenhage_tania_jesus_labor_pain.html.

25 Rae, "Travail of God," 54.

26 André Feuillet, "L'heure de la femme (Jn 16,21) et l'heure de la Mére de Jésus (Jn 19,25-27)," *Biblica* 47 (1966): 169–84. So also John Marsh, *Saint John* (Harmondsworth: Penguin, 1968), 544.

27 Raymond E. Brown, *The Gospel According to John* (2 vols.; Garden City, N.Y.: Doubleday, 1970), 732.

28 Rae, "Travail of God," 57.

29 Rae makes this exegetical and theological move in "Travail of God," 58.

2: Speaking the Labor of God

1 Bertrand Russell and Alfred North Whitehead coauthored the *Principia Mathematica* (vol. 1; Cambridge: Cambridge University Press, 1910) in the second decade of the twentieth century. Their goal was to anchor mathematics in a formal logic.

2 So A. J. Ayer, *Language, Truth, and Logic* (London: Victor Gallancz), 1936.

3 The major works critiquing the nature of and exposing actual practices within the natural sciences are Thomas Kuhn, *The Structure of Scientific Revolutions* (Chicago: University of Chicago Press, 1962); Michael Polanyi, *Personal Knowledge: Towards a Post-critical Philosophy* (London: Routledge, 1958); Imre Lakatos, *Proofs and Refutations: The Logic of Mathematical Discovery* (Cambridge: Cambridge University Press, 1976); Karl Popper, *The Logic of Scientific Discovery* (London: Hutchinson, 1952).

4 Janet Martin Soskice (*Metaphor and Religious Language* [Oxford: Clarendon, 1985], 103–4) complains of this very thing in relation to, e.g., Ian Ramsey (*Models and Mystery* [Oxford: Oxford University Press, 1964]) and Frederick Ferré (*Language, Logic, and God* [London: Eyre & Spottiswoode, 1962]).

5 See especially Basil Mitchell, *Faith and Logic: Oxford Essays in Philosophical Theology* (Boston: Beacon, 1957); Ian Ramsey, *Religious Language: An Empirical Placing of Theological Phrases* (New York: Macmillan, 1957); and Ferré, *Language, Logic, and God*.

6 So Ferré's critique of Ayer's narrow definition of "facts" as scientifically verifiable phenomena (*Language, Logic, and God*, 42–45).

7 Ian Barbour, *Myths, Models, and Paradigms: A Comparative Study in Science and Religion* (New York: Harper & Row, 1974), 37–38.

8 Soskice, *Metaphor*, 122–23.

9 Not everyone, of course, will be satisfied with this assumption. J. Muis' sparkling essay "The Truth of Metaphorical God-Talk" (*SJT* 63 [2010]: 146–62) adequately demonstrates that the self-revealing God is in fact the truth-condition of God-talk and the witness provided by the Christian Scriptures

to God's history with the world functions as the truth-criterion. As Muis notes, the Bible "is itself highly diverse and complex," and, for the canon to function as a proper truth-criterion, "the coherence and unity of the biblical witness about God" must "be made explicit and defined" (162). My own take is that this task is simply monumental and, if the proposed "biblical theologies" of the past century have been any indicator, hopeless. However, that it is in principle possible should assuage any undue worries. In any case it is not, for us, a hill worth dying on.

10 Colin Gunton, *The Actuality of the Atonement: A Study of Metaphor, Rationality, and the Christian Tradition* (London: T&T Clark, 1988), 105.

11 Gunton, *Actuality*, 34.

12 Our treatment of the field metaphor should not be conflated with Wolfhart Pannenberg's pneumatological appropriation. Pannenberg wants to adopt field theory as a linguistic probe into divine action—ostensibly at the quantum level—and as an image for the ontological composition of the Trinity. He is less interested in the philosophy of language at this point and more interested in how the physical sciences and systematic theology might be put into dialogue (see "The Doctrine of Creation and Modern Science," in *Toward a Theology of Nature: Essays on Science and Faith* [ed. Wolfhart Pannenberg and Ted Peters; Louisville, Ky.: Westminster John Knox, 1993], 30–49).

13 Michael Faraday, "10 November, 1845," in *Diary* (vol. 4; London: G. Bell & Sons, 1933), 331.

14 John Dryden, *The Works of John Dryden* (vol. 8; Berkeley: University of California Press, 1965), 144.

15 For some options for the ontological realist, see Johannes Röhl, "Ontological Categories for Fields and Waves," *LNI* (2013): 1866–74.

16 Colin McGinn, *Basic Structures of Reality: Essays on Meta-physics* (Oxford: Oxford University Press, 2011), 137–38.

17 McGinn, *Basic Structures*.

18 Gunton, *Actuality*, 31.

19 Richard Boyd, "Metaphor and Theory Change," in *Metaphor and Thought* (ed. Andrew Ortony; Cambridge: Cambridge University Press, 1979), 371.

20 Gunton, *Actuality*, 45.

21 It should be noted that in this matter, Gunton flirts with Soskice's language but, in effect, rejects her conclusions. Gunton is a Trinitarian first; he approaches theology in general and atonement in particular from the assumption of a Trinity acting perichoretically in the world. So his starting point is the action of God, in this case the life and death of Jesus, and the witnesses to these events as they have been mediated to us in scriptural texts. The metaphors used by Paul and other New Testament writers have been passed down to us as testimonies and responses to what has already been made known (in resurrection) as divine action in history. Gunton does not (contra the argument of Douglas Knight in "From Metaphor to Mediation: Colin Gunton and the Concept of Mediation," *Neue Zeitschrift für Systematische Theologie und Religionsphilosophie* 43 [2001]: 118–36, esp. 130–31)

suggest that metaphors give human beings a way to transfer knowledge from the unknown regions of the divine life into our physical world. This is to get Gunton's Trinitarian approach backward. Metaphors are the human linguistic reactions to the event of God's self-revelation. This observation accords nicely with the critique of Soskice in J. Muis, "Truth of Metaphorical God-Talk," 158–59.

22 Boyd, "Metaphor and Theory Change," 371.

23 As Gunton puts it, "May it not be that, far from the metaphors being mainly or simply projections from standard to theological use, the reverse is true, in the sense that the theological use operates normatively and so alters the meaning of the word in its everyday use?" (*Actuality*, 50–51).

24 See especially Ian Ramsey, *Models and Mystery*, 10, where he follows Max Black's early, largely analogical account of metaphor (see Black, "Metaphor," *Proceedings of the Aristotelian Society* 55 [1954]: 273–94.).

25 Terrence Tilley's sympathetic account ("Ian Ramsey and Empirical Fit," *JAAR* 45 [1977]: 963–88) goes some way toward offsetting the criticisms offered by James Wm. McClendon Jr. and James M. Smith's "qualified appreciation" ("Ian Ramsey's Model of Religious Language: A Qualified Appreciation," *JAAR* 41 [1973]: 413–24) with respect to the clarity and usefulness of Ramsey's theory of justifying religious statements.

26 Soskice, *Metaphor*, 114.

27 Mary Hesse (*Models and Analogies in Science* [Notre Dame, Ind.: Notre Dame University Press, 1966], 30) develops this idea at some length.

28 Max Black, *Models and Metaphors* (Ithaca, N.Y.: Cornell University Press, 1962), 237. Cf. Barbour, *Myths*, 4; Paul Ricoeur, "Metaphor and Reference," in *The Rule of Metaphor: Multidisciplinary Studies in the Creation of Meaning in Language* (trans. Robert Czerny; New York: Routledge, 2003), 289.

29 Using the language of "worlds" anticipates our argument, as it invokes some of Ricoeur's work (analyzed below).

30 The following proceeds according to Hesse's categories: positive, negative, and neutral analogies (*Models and Analogies*, 8).

31 Soskice, *Metaphor*, 48.

32 Ricoeur, *Rule of Metaphor*, 231.

33 See especially Ricoeur's handling of the visual metaphor and Aristotle's account of literature (*Rule of Metaphor*, 231). Aristotle describes a particular class of metaphors that "se[t] [things] before the eyes" as "represent[ing] things in a state of activity" (*Rhet.* 3, 1411b 24–25 [Freese LCL]). Aristotle uses ἐνεργοῦντα ("activity"; note that, contra Freese's translation, the explicit use of the language of movement and direction pushes us to "activity" rather than "actuality") to express the ability of the poet to depict everything—including inanimate objects—as living and moving. Ricoeur appears to suggest that something analogous takes place in every case of semantic shock.

34 Ricoeur, *Rule of Metaphor*, 28, 38.

35 Ricoeur notes that the poet's "elegance" and "urbanity" is his ability to "make discourse appear to the senses" (*Rule of Metaphor*, 38). Just as the inanimate

object is made to be living and moving, so metaphor fuses nonimagistic qualities and associations.

36 Ricoeur, *Rule of Metaphor*, 224.

37 Soskice suggests that if a metaphor is truly reducible, it is no metaphor at all. If it must be classified, it is probably satire or allegory (*Metaphor*, 48–49).

38 Ricoeur, *Rule of Metaphor*, 287.

39 Ricoeur, *Rule of Metaphor*, 13.

40 Ricoeur, *Rule of Metaphor*, 288.

41 Ricoeur, *Rule of Metaphor*, 289. In the quotation I have replaced two technical terms, *lexis* and *muthos*, with the interpretive glosses "individual metaphors" and "the entire plot." This is unfair to Ricoeur in a number of ways, but for the purposes of our present inquiry it must suffice. By *lexis*, Ricoeur typically wants to refer to—in modern parlance—the illocutionary force of the entire expression. So, in the metaphor "My love is a tree," *lexis* could not be reduced to any or all of the individual words. Instead, borrowing from Ricoeur's own notes quoting D. W. Lucas (Aristotle, *Poetics* [trans. D. W. Lucas; Oxford: Clarendon, 1968], 109), *lexis* "covers the whole process of combining words into an intelligible sequence." Rather than delving into a syntactic/semiotic analysis, I think our purposes are better served by my gloss "individual metaphors." As for *muthos*, Ricoeur usually leaves this as a technical term rather than translating it as "fable" or "plot" in order to highlight its mutual interdependence on the mimetic or "redescriptive" or "imitative" aspect of a piece of literature. That is, the plot is purely an act of organizational creation by the author. Those poetic elements that the author "borrows from the world" (human intentions, character, personality, etc.) intersect with the plot and imbue it (as it would otherwise be merely invention) with the essence of the real world. See Ricoeur's essay "Between Rhetoric," in *Rule of Metaphor*, 13–27.

42 Robert W. Jenson, *Canon and Creed* (Louisville, Ky.: Westminster John Knox, 2010), 20.

3: Converting the Cross

1 Cynthia S. W. Crysdale, *Embracing Travail* (New York: Continuum, 2001), 2.

2 Cf. Michaels, *Gospel of John*, 844, who notes that John's Gospel was certainly written by a man.

3 René Girard, *Violence and the Sacred* (trans. Patrick Gregory; Baltimore: Johns Hopkins University Press, 1977); the work first appeared in French as *La Violence et le sacré* (Paris: Editions Bernard Grasset, 1972).

4 Mark S. Heim, *Saved from Sacrifice: A Theology of the Cross* (Grand Rapids: Eerdmans, 2006).

5 Heim, *Saved from Sacrifice*, 64.

6 René Girard, *I See Satan Fall like Lightning* (trans. James G. Williams; Maryknoll, N.Y.: Orbis, 2001), 148.

7 Robert Nozick, "Coercion," in *Philosophy, Science, and Method: Essays in Honor of Ernest Nagel* (ed. S. Morgenbesser, P. Suppes, and M. White; New York: St. Martin's, 1969), 440–72.

8 J. Denny Weaver, *The Nonviolent Atonement* (Grand Rapids: Eerdmans, 2001), 9. It is worth noting that the introduction into popular discourse of "nudging" (e.g., Cass R. Sunstein and Richard H. Thaler, *Nudge: Improving Decisions about Health, Wealth, and Happiness* [New Haven: Yale University Press, 2008]) is something like an attempt to reclaim a positive notion of coercion.

9 Weaver, *Nonviolent Atonement*, 9.

10 Walter Wink, *Engaging the Powers: Discernment and Resistance in a World of Domination* (Minneapolis: Fortress, 1992), 192.

11 Weaver, *Nonviolent Atonement*, 36.

12 Martin Hengel's now-classic *Crucifixion* (trans. John Bowden; Philadelphia: Fortress, 1977) demonstrates the roles of shame and exclusion in the horror of death-by-the-cross.

13 We use the word "violence" intentionally here (rather than, say, "damage"). The kind of abrupt physical change made by the birth process would, under nonbirthing circumstances, be violent. Yet it is because what is happening is the birth of a human child and not torture that the physical damage does not hinder Godward transformation.

14 Frederick Dale Bruner, *The Gospel of John: A Commentary* (Grand Rapids: Eerdmans, 2012).

15 The Hebrew underlying "gasp and pant" in v. 14b is notoriously difficult; *š'p* and the *hapax legomenon nšm* offer a number of possibilities. The LXX, Targum, and Vulgate all assume that *nšm* is related to *šmm* ("to be made desolate") and therefore not a *hapax* at all. The ancient sources thus render v. 14b as the rough equivalent of the pairing of these verbs in Ezekiel 36:3, meaning something along the lines of "I will desolate and crush" (so John Goldingay and David Payne, *A Critical and Exegetical Commentary on Isaiah 40–55* [vol. 1; New York: T&T Clark, 2006], 246). Meyer Gruber ("The Motherhood of God in Second Isaiah," *RB* 90 [1983]: 351–59) adopts the translation "I will inhale and exhale simultaneously," explicitly suggesting that the prophet anticipates what we think of today as Lamaze breathing (354–55n11). Gruber's argument rightly emphasizes Second Isaiah's multiple uses of the God-as-Mother metaphor (42:14b; 49:15a), noting that in this prophet at least, "in natural childbirth the woman's role is active rather than passive" (355). On the weight of this argument about Second Isaiah as a discrete piece of literature, the NRSV's "gasp and pant" is marginally preferable to Goldingay's translation.

16 Treating Isaiah as a literary and conceptual whole now enjoys a budding heritage in the academy. See John D. W. Watts, *Isaiah 1–33* (Waco, Tex.: Word, 1985); idem, *Isaiah 34–66* (Waco, Tex.: Word, 1987); Brevard Childs, *Isaiah: A Commentary* (Louisville, Ky.: Westminster John Knox, 2001).

17 Kathryn Pfisterrer Darr ("Two Unifying Female Images in the Book of Isa-
    iah," in *Uncovering Ancient Stones: Essays in Memory of H. Neil Richard-
    son* [ed. L. M. Hopfe; Winona Lake, Ind.: Eisenbrauns, 1994], 17–18) even
    suggests that the pervasive use of female imagery bolsters Barry Webb's
    argument for treating Isaiah as a whole (Webb, "Zion in Transformation: A
    Literary Approach to Isaiah," in *The Bible in Three Dimensions: Essays in
    Honor of Forty Years of Biblical Studies in the University of Sheffield* [ed. D. J.
    A. Clines et al.; Sheffield: JSOT Press, 1992], 65–84).

18 Darr, "Female Images," 23.

19 Kathryn Pfisterrer Darr, "Like Warrior, Like Woman: Destruction and Deliv-
    erance in Isaiah 42:10-17," *CBQ* 49 (1987): 560–71.

20 Goldingay and Payne, *Isaiah 40–55*, 247.

21 Contra James Muilenburg ("The Book of Isaiah: Chapters 40–66," in *The
    Interpreter's Bible* [vol. 5; Nashville: Abingdon, 1956], 467–74), whose influ-
    ential interpretation asserts that "the sudden shift" from warrior imagery to
    labor pains is "in the manner of the poet" (473). This might suggest that the
    metaphor is merely ornamental, though, as we shall see, literary context must
    push us in other directions. Cf. Claus Westermann (*Isaiah 40–66* [London:
    SCM Press, 1969], 106), who puts the emphasis on the "change from long
    silence to crying out"; and John Oswalt (*The Book of Isaiah 40–66* [Grand
    Rapids: Eerdmans, 1998], 125), who discerns the similarity between the king
    and labor similes to be "the outcry at the climactic moment."

22 Darr, "Like Warrior, Like Woman," 571.

23 Other occurrences of our simile (Micah 4:9, 10) express the same theme,
    as do closely related forms in Isaiah 21:3; Hosea 13:13; Micah 5:2; cf. Darr,
    "Like Warrior, Like Woman," 565–66.

24 C. S. Lewis, *A Grief Observed* (London: Faber, 1961), 45.

25 Eberhard Jüngel, *God as the Mystery of the World: On the Foundation of the
    Theology of the Crucified One in the Dispute between Theism and Atheism*
    (trans. Darrell L. Guder; Grand Rapids: Eerdmans, 1983).

26 Jüngel, *God as the Mystery of the World*, 184; cf. 199–225.

27 Jüngel, *God as the Mystery of the World*, 219; emphasis added.

28 Jüngel, *God as the Mystery of the World*, 219–20.

29 Nevertheless, a few have recently taken up the monumental challenge of
    defending classical notions of impassibility. While we will not entertain the
    arguments here, it is worth mentioning several full-length treatments. See
    Thomas G. Weinandy, *Does God Suffer?* (Notre Dame, Ind.: University of
    Notre Dame Press, 2000); and Daniel Castelo, *The Apathetic God: Exploring
    the Contemporary Relevance of Divine Impassibility* (Eugene, Ore.: Wipf &
    Stock, 2009).

30 Jürgen Moltmann, *The Crucified God* (trans. R. A. Wilson and John Bowden;
    Minneapolis: Fortress, 1993), 151–52.

31 The potential implications are in fact legion and have been discussed else-
    where at length. For the most prominent critique, see Weinandy, *Does God
    Suffer?* especially 152–71. Paul S. Fiddes' *The Creative Suffering of God*

(Oxford: Clarendon, 1992) develops the theme of divine suffering system-atically, attending to issues of time, eternity, and the integrity of the divine persons.

32   Creation and redemption have been—and should be—tightly related doc-trines, though the theological direction, as it were, has tended to be one way: a theological reckoning of creation produces particular characterizations of redemption. This makes sense as far as it goes, for how would we know what the incarnation, cross, and resurrection accomplish without some robust account either of what has been lost or of what telos the cosmos possessed at inception? The labor metaphor, however, pushes theology in the other direc-tion; a fresh reckoning of the cross helps us reconsider creation in a new light, drawing out insights that may previously have been missed.

33   John Milbank, "'I Will Gasp and Pant': Deutero-Isaiah and the Birth of the Suffering Subject," *Semeia* 59 (1992): 59–71.

34   So Goldingay and Payne (*Isaiah 40–55*, 247). Muilenburg ("Book of Isaiah," in vol. 5 of *The Interpreter's Bible*, 473), Phyllis Trible (*God and the Rhetoric of Sexuality* [Philadelphia: Fortress, 1978], 64), and Gruber ("Motherhood of God," 354–55) contend that the offspring should be understood as a "new cre-ation," but they fail to reckon with the labor simile's subordination to the war-rior simile. That is, even if we reject Goldingay's translation of v. 14b, retaining the "gasping and panting" of a woman in labor, what plainly follows in v. 15 is the warrior's destruction, the "laying waste to mountains and hills." Faithful-ness to the co-text pushes our imaging of the birth metaphor in this direction.

35   Milbank, "Gasp and Pant," 67.

36   Translation adapted from John Goldingay, *Psalms 90–150* (Grand Rapids: Baker Academic, 2008), 25.

37   See, e.g., Marvin Tate, *Psalms 51–100* (Dallas: Word, 1990), 440–41; cf. Hans-Joachim Kraus, *Psalms 60–150: A Commentary* (Minneapolis: Augs-burg, 1989), 215, where the metaphors in v. 2 "contradict the faith in cre-ation"; Goldingay, *Psalms 90–150*, 25–26.

38   See, e.g., Marianne Grohmann, "Metaphors of God, Nature and Birth," in *Metaphors in the Psalms* (ed. Pierre van Hecke and Antje Labahn; Leu-ven: Uitgeverij Peeters, 2010), 28; Julia A. Foster, "The Use of *ḥyl* as God-Language in the Hebrew Scriptures," in *Uncovering Ancient Stones: Essays in Memory of H. Neil Richardson* (ed. Lewis M. Hopfe; Winona Lake, Ind.: Eisenbrauns, 1994), 93–94, 101–2.

39   See, e.g., Konrad Schaefer, *Psalms* (Collegeville, Minn.: Liturgical, 2001), 225–27; cf. Matthias Köckert's interpretation of Psalm 90 in light of the phys-ics of space-time ("Zeit und Ewigkeit in Psalm 90," in *Zeit und Ewigkeit als Raum göttlichen Handelns: Religionsgeschichtliche, theologische und philos-ophische Perspektiven* [ed. Reinhard G. Kratz and Hermann Spieckermann; Berlin: de Gruyter, 2009], 155–85). Köckert makes special mention of the experiential aspect of our plight over and against God's eternality (see esp. 174–77); see also Patrick D. Miller, *Interpreting the Psalms* (Philadelphia: Fortress, 1986), 126–27.

40 Cf. Köckert, "Zeit und Ewigkeit," 174–75.

41 Köckert ("Zeit und Ewigkeit," 177) contrasts the "almost serene" ("beinahe abgeklärten") vv. 11-12 with the "emotional outcry" ("emotionalen Aufsch- rei") that begins the third section of the psalm in v. 13.

42 See, e.g., Jon D. Levinson, *Creation and the Persistence of Evil: The Jewish Drama of Divine Omnipotence* (Princeton, N.J.: Princeton University Press, 1988), preface.

43 J. Richard Middleton (*The Liberating Image: The* Imago Dei *in Genesis 1* [Grand Rapids: Brazos, 2005], 236–40) traces *Chaoskampf* scholarship from Gunkel in the late nineteenth century to the present day.

44 Middleton, *Liberating Image*, 264.

45 Middleton, *Liberating Image*, 265.

46 Athanasius, *De incarnatione*, §1.

47 Karl Barth writes, "Jesus Christ was in the beginning with God" (*CD* II/2, 104). This claim may suggest that Barth denies the doctrine of the *Logos Asarkos* ("Word without flesh"): that somehow the Second Person of the Trinity is the man Jesus of Nazareth from eternity. On its face this appears absurd, though a number of novel solutions have been suggested (see the review of positions in Edwin Chr. van Driel, "Karl Barth and the Eternal Existence of Jesus Christ," *SJT* 60 [2007]: 45–61). At the very least we can suggest that Barth must con- ceive of the Godhead knowing the incarnation anticipatorily from eternity, that the divine triune being and the divine act of cosmic election are both from eternity. As such, the temporal experience of crucifixion is—at the very least—"anticipated" or "expected" in God's being "before" creation. We use the quotes to point out the necessity of metaphors when we deploy temporal verbs to describe a nature and act that are, by definition, not subjected to tem- porality except insofar as it is God's nature and act to be and do such.

48 This does not entail—or really even imply—an endlessly suffering, eternally dying god since the Word is but one person of the Trinity. The Word's eternal self-abnegation, the "localizing nothingness" in God's being, issues in the procession of the life-giving Spirit. As we will argue in chapter 6 below, the Spirit proceeds "through the Son," which is to say that in God's immanent being the Spirit comes through the Word's pathos, issuing in vivification. This, as Jüngel points out, is love: self-abnegation for the sake of bringing life to the other.

49 John Goldingay, *After Eating the Apricot* (Carlisle, UK: Paternoster, 1996), 19– 20; and see also Goldingay's paper "Re-reading Eve and Adam," n.p., accessed 7 May 2014, http://infoguides.fuller.edu/c.php?g=567517&p=3909099; cf. R. W. L. Moberly, "Did the Serpent Get It Right?" *JTS* 39 (1988): 1–27 (esp. 17–18).

4: Birthing the Church

1 Ian A. McFarland, *In Adam's Fall: A Meditation on the Christian Doctrine of Original Sin* (West Sussex: Wiley-Blackwell, 2010), 8.

2   Mark E. Biddle, *Missing the Mark: Sin and Its Consequences in Biblical Theology* (Nashville: Abingdon, 2005), 117.

3   Biddle, *Missing the Mark*, 119.

4   Cf. Rolf Knierim, *Die Hauptbegriffe fuer Suende im Alten Testament* (Gütersloh: Mohn, 1965), 239–43.

5   Dietrich Bonhoeffer, *Ethics* (trans. Neville Horton Smith; New York: Macmillan, 1955), 22.

6   Bonhoeffer, *Ethics*, 190.

7   Josiah Young ("Dietrich Bonhoeffer and Reinhold Niebuhr: Their Ethics, Views on Karl Barth, and Perspectives on African Americans," in *Bonhoeffer's Intellectual Formation: Theology and Philosophy in His Thought* [ed. Peter Frick; Tübingen: Mohr Siebeck, 2008], 283–300) helpfully contrasts Bonhoeffer and his one-time teacher on the issues of origins and ultimate ends. He explains, "Niebuhr's concern was how '*man*' should think about himself in relation to God and the world while Bonhoeffer's and Barth's concern was how *God* thinks about humankind in relation to Godself and the world" (290; emphasis in original).

8   The "I" of Romans 7 has been a flashpoint in Pauline exegesis. Colin Kruse (*Paul's Letter to the Romans* [Grand Rapids: Eerdmans, 2012], 314–20) offers a review and short analysis of the relevant positions. Kruse, like Paul Trudinger ("An Autobiographical Digression? A Note on Romans 7:7-25," *ExpTim* 107 [1996]: 173) and N. T. Wright (*Paul and the Faithfulness of God* [Minneapolis: Fortress, 2013], 892–94; idem, "Romans," in *The New Interpreter's Bible: Acts–1 Corinthians* [ed. Leander Keck; Nashville: Abingdon, 2002], 562–72), argues that Paul is here using the rhetorical device of "speech-in-character" to offer a theological analysis of Israel's past and present state (thus making sense of the switch from the aorist to the present in vv. 12-14). The deciding factor in favor of this reading is the fact that it makes Paul's argument coherent and noncontradictory, specifically with respect to the role of the Spirit in the life of Christians. If Paul uses "I" to refer to Christian experience in ch. 7, then he is explicitly contradicting his pronouncement to the Roman Christians about freedom from sin in 6:14. We are happy to suggest that the "I" may be applied to all non-Christian paganism that encounters Judaism, but the primary context must be Israel, as it is the relationship of a people to Torah that is in view.

9   See Peter Stuhlmacher, *Paul's Letter to the Romans: A Commentary* (Louisville, Ky.: Westminster John Knox, 1994), 109. The translation of the Community Rule is my own.

10 Beverly Roberts Gaventa ("The Cosmic Power of Sin in Paul's Letter to the Romans: Toward a Widescreen Edition," *Int* 58 [2004]: 229–40) takes this sort of thinking to its logical extreme, capitalizing the "S" in "Sin" and reconfiguring it as a cosmic power.

11 James D. G. Dunn, *Romans 1–8* (Dallas: Word, 1988), 400.

12 Not all will agree. Douglas Moo ("Sin in Paul," in *Fallen: A Theology of Sin* [ed. Christopher W. Morgan and Robert A. Peterson; Wheaton, Ill.: Crossway,

2013], 107–30), for example, castigates those who "think that this language suggests that Paul views sin as an evil spiritual power, a kind of demon," for "this would be to mistake personification for personalization." Paul does not actually think sin has personal qualities; rather, he "attributes personal qualities to sin in order to vividly picture the power and devastating effects of human sin in the lives of human beings" (111). Ironically, Moo's own exposition of Paul's hamartiology cannot proceed without writing as if sin possesses a kind of agency. Thus, e.g., sin "co-opt[s] God's law for its own purposes" (113). We should note that in this Moo is just following Paul's example, as in Romans 7:8 in which sin "seizes an opportunity." It is hard to know what to make of Moo's kind of thinking, as it acknowledges the diversity and depth of sin language in Scripture and yet insists that it all can be reduced to the individual committing a "violation of God's law, covenant, or will" (see John W. Mahony, "A Theology of Sin for Today," 187–217 [193] in the same edited volume).

13 Mark J. Boda, *A Severe Mercy: Sin and Its Remedy in the Old Testament* (Winona Lake, Ind.: Eisenbrauns, 2009), 11.

14 Boda, *Severe Mercy*, 429, exegeting Psalm 51:12-14.

15 Compare Ben Witherington III's treatment (*The Acts of the Apostles: A Socio-rhetorical Commentary* [Grand Rapids: Eerdmans, 1997], 218), where Ananias and Sapphira's unity "violated the togetherness of the community," and contrast with Darrell Bock's reading (*Acts* [Grand Rapids: Baker, 2007], 219), where the issue is violating a command of God—namely, lying,—or David G. Peterson's interpretation (*The Acts of the Apostles* [Grand Rapids: Eerdmans, 2009], 93), where judgment "exposes those who do not truly belong" to the community. Also see Gerd Theissen's *The Miracle Stories of the Early Christian Tradition* ([trans. Francis McDonagh; Minneapolis: Fortress, 1982], 109), where he takes the story of Ananias and Sapphira as a New Testament token of "rule miracles of punishment," in which a punitive sign confirms a prophetic word of judgment.

16 The NRSV reads "the water of rebirth." I have substituted the more literal "washing" (λουτροῦ; cf. TNIV, CEB) to distance the English from sacramental overtones. This is not to suggest that baptism is not in view. It is rather to emphasize the role of the Spirit as the one doing the washing. Whether washing takes place at baptism or baptism is meant to signal that washing has taken place, it is the Spirit—not the water—that has effected "rebirth and renewal."

17 Philip Towner (*The Letters to Timothy and Titus* [Grand Rapids: Eerdmans, 2006], 768–86) points out the relevant echoes, arguing persuasively that the entire section recalls "a catena of Ezekiel texts" (784) and that these are primarily Spirit-texts. When read from the perspective of Ezekiel, the cosmic and pneumatological nature of the echoes of Psalm 104 and Joel 2 come to the forefront.

18 Towner, *Letters to Timothy and Titus*, 762.

19 Towner, *Letters to Timothy and Titus*, 763.

20 Towner, *Letters to Timothy and Titus*, 764. For Towner, "fulfillment of Torah" takes center stage in the salvific theology of the letter. "Justification," Towner's traditional translation of the single instance of δικαιόω and its cognates in Titus, is given a sort of interpretive primacy. It is difficult to say why this should be, given that he assiduously points out the many metaphors the author deploys to explain spiritual realities. It might be that a prior commitment to something like Lutheran justification is in play, for how else should we explain his insistence that "the legal decision," that is, "justification" (3:7), should result in "becoming heirs" (787)? If this is correct, it might explain why Towner is so quick to reduce the Spirit's role to a kind of special empowering. The theological heavy lifting, as it were, has already been done in the status change from guilty to justified; it is now the believer working in concert with the Spirit that produces sanctification. We are at pains here to suggest that such a view undervalues the metaphors in Titus and the Old Testament texts from which they are drawn.

21 Towner calls them "almost synonymous" (*Letters to Timothy and Titus*, 781), though it is difficult to discern any substantive manner in which they are not synonymous on his view.

22 So, e.g., Towner, *Letters to Timothy and Titus*, 787, where he states that the heir metaphor of Titus 3:7 refers to believers "having received the verdict of acquittal or vindication."

23 The textual link is admittedly not as strong as the conceptual link. This partly explains why few commentators make much of the psalm other than to note the echo.

24 Jürgen Moltmann, *God in Creation: A New Theology of Creation and the Spirit of God* (trans. Margaret Kohl; Minneapolis: Fortress, 1993), 10.

25 Water, possibly indicating baptism, accompanies new birth, as does renewal by the Holy Spirit. Christiane Zimmerman argues that παλιγγενεσίας should be rendered "regeneration" ("Wiederentstehung") in order to account for the Pauline tradition of cosmic renewal and the influence of Philo's stoicism ("Wiederentstehung und Erneuerung [Tit 3:5]: Zu einem erhaltenswerten Aspekt der Soteriologie des Titusbriefs," *NovT* 51 [2009]: 272–95). Zimmerman is right to move the discussion away from Käsemann's emphasis on rebirth in the pagan mystery cults (Käsemann, "Titus 3:4-7," in *Exegetische Versuche und Besinnungen I* [Göttingen: Vandenhoeck & Ruprecht, 1965], 299), but removing the language of birth entirely goes a bridge too far. Zimmerman's interest in countering the hyperindividualistic soteriology championed by Käsemann does not require drastic retranslation. Paul's use of birth language in Romans 8, perhaps the single most cosmically oriented soteriological discourse in the Pauline corpus, should quell Zimmerman's concerns. As we note above, the real emphasis should be placed on the New Testament's (and Paul's!) repeated juxtaposition of new/second birth and the Spirit.

26 For a review of the various positions, see Robert Yarbrough, *1–3 John* (Grand Rapids: Baker Academic, 2008), 194–95; see also Raymond E. Brown, *The Epistles of John: Translated with Introduction, Notes, and Commentary* (New

York: Doubleday, 1982), 409; cf. J. de Waal Dryden, "The Sense of σπέρμα in 1 John 3:9 in Light of the Lexical Evidence," *EFN* 11 (1998): 85–100.

27 Neil Alexander comments, "The fact that it makes John tautologous need not argue against its probability!" (*The Epistles of John: Introduction and Commentary* [London: SCM Press, 1962], 86–87): an amusing observation, but fundamentally wrongheaded. John Spencer Hill ("τὰ βαΐα τῶ φοινίκων [John 12:13]: Pleonasm or Prolepsis?" *JBL* 101 [1982]: 133–35) notes in an entirely different context that there is a strong possibility that βαΐα, which can signify either "palm" or "phoenix," might be a Johannine literary allusion rather than a poorly worded phrase ("the large crowd . . . took the palm/phoenix branches of palm trees"). The phoenix echo, prominent in early Christian reflection on resurrection, makes sense of the bizarre diction without resorting to denigrating the author's literary prowess. We bring up this somewhat obscure observation to point out a larger interpretive rule: Johannine material that appears to be tautologous on first blush is much more likely to have literary depth. It is highly associative; it points to other common themes and tropes. Dismissing Johannine syntax as repetitive and simple is potentially to miss the texture of a rich literary world.

28 Charles H. Dodd, *Johannine Epistles* (London: Harper & Row, 1946), 77.

29 Rudolph Schnackenburg, *The Johannine Epistles* (New York: Crossroad, 1992), 175.

30 Colin Kruse (*The Letters of John* [Grand Rapids: Eerdmans, 2000], 124–26) appeals to grammatical structure, namely, a chiasm in 3:9, of which "because God's seed remains in you" is the middle, to emphasize the ethical import here. Ultimately, Kruse opts to read "seed" as the indwelling of the Holy Spirit, but, whatever the seed may be, its presence categorically excludes sin, or on Kruse's reading, factionalism/rebellion.

31 Incidentally, BDAG lists "genetic material" as a possible meaning for σπέρμα, even citing 1 John 3:9 as the paradigm example in the New Testament. For the argument in favor of this specific interpretation, see John Painter, "The 'Opponents' in 1 John," *NTS* 32 (1986): 48–71. Note also that the CEB just translates the term as "DNA." Cf. Reinhard Feldmeier, *The First Letter of Peter: A Commentary on the Greek Text* (trans. Peter H. Davids; Waco, Tex.: Baylor University Press, 2008), 130. Feldmeier is careful to note that any instance of the metaphor should be treated in its native literary context, but his comments are apropos in light of the logic of 1 John.

32 Michaels, *Gospel of John*, 185.

33 François Ansermet and Pierre Magistretti, *Biology of Freedom: Neural Plasticity, Experience, and the Unconscious* (trans. Susan Fairfield; London: Karnac, 2007), 182.

34 For extended reflections on this, see Paul Markham, *Rewired: Exploring Religious Conversion* (Eugene, Ore.: Wipf & Stock, 2007), especially chs. 4 ("Rewired") and 5 ("A Sanctifying Community").

35 Giacomo Rizzolatti and Maddalena Fabbri-Destro, "The Mirror Mechanism: Understanding Others from the Inside," in *Understanding Other Minds:*

Perspectives from Developmental Social Neuroscience (ed. Simon Baron-Cohen, Helen Tager-Flusberg, and Michael V. Lombardo; Oxford: Oxford University Press, 2013), 264–90.

36   Rizzolatti and Fabbri-Destro, "Mirror Mechanism," 282.

5: Transcending Exchange

1   Cf. Mark D. Baker and Joel B. Green, *Recovering the Scandal of the Cross: Atonement in New Testament and Contemporary Contexts* (2nd ed.; Downers Grove, Ill.: InterVarsity, 2011), 73–74. We will leave to the side the prior question about how, if Christians confess a triune God, we can even picture the death of the Son as the Father perpetrating violence against an entirely different person. One suspects that accusations of tritheism are not far in the offing on this view.

2   Stephen Finlan, *Problems with Atonement* (Collegeville, Minn.: Liturgical, 2005), 8–9.

3   Finlan, *Problems with Atonement*, 9.

4   See chapter 2 above.

5   J. Denny Weaver's narrative *Christus Victor* claims to be more than a species of moral influence—and it is, except with respect to the cross. His verbs tell the tale: "The resurrection *reveals* the true balance of power in the universe"; "Jesus' death is . . . the ultimate statement that *distinguishes* the rule of God from the reign of evil" (Weaver, *Nonviolent Atonement*, 45; emphasis added). Weaver's view blends Girardian scapegoating theory and Anabaptist nonviolence with Aulénian classical *Christus Victor* to offer a compelling account in which Jesus' Spirit-led life actively defeats the powers, but his death remains revelatory.

6   Friedrich Nietzsche, *Genealogy of Morals* (trans. Carol Diethe; Cambridge: Cambridge University Press, 1994), especially pp. 62–63.

7   Nietzsche, *Genealogy of Morals*, 63; emphasis original.

8   Nietzsche, *Genealogy of Morals*, 63.

9   See, e.g., Jacques Derrida, *Given Time: I. Counterfeit Money* (trans. Peggy Kamuf; Chicago: University of Chicago Press, 1992); idem, *The Gift of Death* (trans. David Wills; Chicago: University of Chicago Press, 1995); idem, "On the Gift: A Discussion between Jacques Derrida and Jean-Luc Marion," in *God, the Gift, and Postmodernism* (ed. John D. Caputo and Michael J. Scanlon; Bloomington: Indiana University Press, 1999), 54–78.

10   Derrida, *Given Time*, 14.

11   James Laidlaw ("A Free Gift Makes No Friends," in *The Question of the Gift: Essays across Disciplines* [ed. Mark Osteen; New York: Routledge, 2002], 45–66) reviews the practices of "renouncers" and lay practitioners of Shvetambar Jainism in India. The renouncers rely entirely on the gifts of the laypeople, but the ritual practices of almsgiving and hospitality are systematically purged of the economies of reciprocity that ought to result. Laidlaw offers the relationship between renouncers and lay Jainists partially to

counter the widely accepted Nietzschean anthropological view—articulated in modern research by Chris Gregory (*Gifts and Commodities* [London: Academic Press, 1982])—that there are "no real gifts in anthropology." In the end Laidlaw concedes that even the radical practices of the Shvetambar Jainists do not measure up to true giftedness, and that in human societies, "almost nothing ever could" (63).

12 Dunn, *Romans 1–8*, 348; Douglas Moo, *The Epistle to the Romans* (Grand Rapids: Eerdmans, 1996), 403.

13 Kevin Vanhoozer, "The Atonement in Postmodernity: Guilt, Goats and Gifts," in *The Glory of the Atonement: Biblical, Historical, and Practical Perspectives* (ed. Charles E. Hill and Frank A. James III; Downers Grove, Ill.: InterVarsity, 2004), 367–403.

14 A number of contemporary translations (e.g., NRSV, CEB) translate χάρισμα as "free gift" rather than just "gift." The choice no doubt arises from the heavy emphasis on grace and graciousness in Romans 1–8.

15 Paul Ricoeur, *The Conflict of Interpretations: Essays in Hermeneutics* (ed. Don Ihde; Evanston, Ill.: Northwestern University Press, 1974), 376.

16 Ricoeur, *Conflict of Interpretations*, 374.

17 It is difficult to judge the extent to which Ricoeur's textual-theological contributions can be classified according to Anglo-American schema. He sometimes (as here) sounds postliberal, creating a kind of doctrinal language game held existentially to be true, though perhaps not referring in the philosophical sense. So it might be that Ricoeur, having traversed the "desert of criticism," does not think that, historically, God actually ever gave Torah or expected it to be followed by human beings. Rather, Torah's value is its textualization and the categories and responses it creates in hearers now. And, perhaps, it is likewise with the gospel news of resurrection. As should be clear in our appropriation, however, Ricoeur's ambiguity on these issues does not blunt the utility of the substance of his theological reflection. For extensive consideration of Ricoeur's value in contemporary constructive theology, see Dan Stiver, *Theology after Ricoeur: New Directions in Hermeneutical Theology* (Louisville, Ky.: Westminster John Knox, 2001).

18 Troels Engberg-Pedersen, "Gift-Giving and Friendship: Seneca and Paul in Romans 1–8 on the Logic of God's χάρις and Its Human Response," *HTR* 101 (2008): 15–44.

19 See chapter 2 above for the discussion of religious metaphors imposing alterations on regular use of language.

20 Wright, *Paul and the Faithfulness of God*, 488.

21 Ricoeur, *Conflict of Interpretations*, 369.

22 Wright, *Paul and the Faithfulness of God*, 890.

23 Wright, *Paul and the Faithfulness of God*, 754.

24 Of course anyone who has lived for any period of time in the church knows that economies of exchange are alive and well and this must be addressed. It is enough for now to identify the true nature and character of the church, her

DNA so to speak, knowing that character may not be fully expressed until the *eschaton*.

25 So it is that describing believers as a "new humanity" or "new race" is insufficient or at least derivative of the familial metaphor. This is true even at the exegetical level in the case of, say, Ephesians 2:11-22 where the new humanity has a familial inheritance (1:14, 18) and comprises the household (οἰκεῖος) of God (2:19, 20). The God-born are no doubt a new kind of humanity, but their "divine ethnicity," if we may put it that way, is drawn from the fact that believers all share the same parents thanks to the labor of the cross.

26 David deSilva notes (*Honor, Patronage, Kinship, and Purity: Unlocking New Testament Culture* [Downers Grove, Ill.: IVP Academic, 2000], 186), following Aristotle, that "children are held to have incurred a debt to their parents that they can never repay." Philo holds children to be "subjects and servants" (*Spec. Laws* 2.227 [Colson LCL]) of their parents. But it must be noted that these mores are enculturated—that is, learned, not innate. A child very quickly recognizes operative norms, but these are not built in. Moreover, deSilva's analysis does not take into account what Caroline Johnson Hodge (*If Sons, Then Heirs: A Study of Kinship and Ethnicity in the Letters of Paul* [Oxford: Oxford University Press, 2007], 21), following Gerd Baumann (*The Multicultural Riddle: Rethinking National, Ethnic, and Religious Identities* [London: Routledge, 1999]), calls "essentialist and processual discourses of culture." Essentialist discourse assumes that there are inherent ties that bind; processual discourses assume that kinship is a social construct. As Johnson Hodge notes, these views are not incompatible but complementary, since "the very act of stating or claiming an essential common bond with other members is itself a construction of identity" (21). Thus, it is the case that children might know themselves as children in an essentialist manner—much in the way that Caesar knows himself to be a son of the gods—before or even alongside a notion of themselves as subject to or indebted to parents. To put it simply, deSilva's observations are not wrong; they are simply incomplete and, as it happens, compatible with the quasiexistentialist account we have given.

6: Expanding the Agony of the Cross

1 J. Gordon McConville, *Being Human in God's World: An Old Testament Theology of Humanity* (Grand Rapids: Baker, 2016), 126.

2 Paul Sanders' *The Provenance of Deuteronomy 32* (Leiden: Brill, 1996) provides a helpful rundown of the relevant arguments. For more recent work involving a complex history-of-interpretation approach, see Otto Eckart, "Moses Abschiedslied in Deuteronomium 32: Ein Zeugnis der Kanonsbildung in der Hebräischen Bibel," in *Die Tora* (Wiesbaden: Harrassowitz, 2009), 641–78; and Mark Leuchter ("Why Is the Song of Moses in the Book of Deuteronomy?" *VT* 57 [2007]: 295–317), who suggests that an analysis of the function of the Song in Deuteronomy might issue in a reasonable redaction history and therefore a plausible date.

With respect to structural concerns, see, e.g., Duane Christensen's three major divisions and multiple subdivisions (*Deuteronomy 21:10–34:12* [Nashville: Nelson, 2002], 783–821). Christensen accepts and expands on the divisions recommended by Patrick W. Skehan, "The Structure of the Song of Moses in Deuteronomy (Dt 32:1-43)," *CBQ* 13 (1951): 153–63. Among other text-critical studies, see I. Himbaza, "Dt 32, 8, une Correction Tardive des Scribes: Essai D'interprétation et de Datation," *Bib* 83 (2002): 527–48; Jan Joosten, "A Note on the Text of Deuteronomy xxxii 8," *VT* 57 (2007): 548–55. Intertextual studies include Thomas A. Keiser, "The Song of Moses a Basis for Isaiah's Prophecy," *VT* 55 (2005): 486–500; Hyun Chul Paul Kim, "The Song of Moses (Deuteronomy 32:1-43) in Isaiah 40–55," in *God's Word for Our World: Biblical Studies in Honor of Simon John De Vries* (vol. 1; ed. J. H. Ellens, D. I. Ellens, R. P. Knierem, and I. Kalimi; New York: T&T Clark, 2004), 147–71. Also pertinent to our topic is Klaus Baltzer's suggestion that the father/mother metaphor in Deuteronomy 32 may help make sense of Isaiah 51, where God is also conceived of as Rock (*Deutero Isaiah* [Hermeneia; Minneapolis: Augsburg, 2001], 346).

3   This is not to say that commentators have not attended—often quite lavishly—to the poetics of the section. See, especially, Christensen, for whom "the text is hauntingly beautiful, even in translation" (*Deuteronomy 21:10–34:12*, 785).

4   For some similar literary reasoning, see Urszula Szwarc, "Skała Izraela w Świetle Wiersza Pwt 32, 18," *Roczniki Teologiczne* 49 (2002): 5–13. I owe the "Rock-Parent" language to Szwarc (especially p. 8).

5   See chapter 3 above.

6   Christensen, *Deuteronomy 21:10–34:12*, 785.

7   On "teaching Israel to fly," see Peter C. Craigie, *The Book of Deuteronomy* (Grand Rapids: Eerdmans, 1976), 381.

8   Nursing, of course, is biologically the domain of the mother. So it is not the case that God is some sort of "super-father," a father who exhibits traits that have been traditionally rendered as maternal. No, God does what is exclusive to mothers, what fathers are incapable of doing. Two corollaries follow: (1) in Deuteronomy 32, God is mother; and (2) Moses' Song does not admit of what contemporary discourse would think of as clear gender roles. Rather, God is pictured as the all-in-all parent, doing all that fathers and mothers can or could or should do in the nurturing and rearing of children.

9   Szwarc, "Skała," 8–9.

10   Michael J. Gorman, *Cruciformity: Paul's Narrative Spirituality of the Cross* (Grand Rapids: Eerdmans, 2001), 52.

11   Gorman, *Cruciformity*, 57.

12   Robert C. Tannehill, *Dying and Rising with Christ: A Study in Pauline Theology* (Berlin: Alfred Töpelmann, 1966), 80. Gorman approvingly cites Tannehill, emphasizing the activity of the believer in this "putting to death of the flesh." That is, our participation, our being "in Christ," is both a gift and work of God and an active choice.

13 Gorman, *Cruciformity*, 55; emphasis original.

14 Wright, *Paul and the Faithfulness of God*, 1259.

15 The identity of the author of 1 Peter is a question about which we may remain agnostic; in places where it is smoother to do so, I have used "Peter" as a name for the author.

16 See Joel B. Green's "Narrating the Gospel in 1 and 2 Peter" (*Int* 60 [2006]: 262–77) for an extensive exploration of how theological time functions in the background to furnish a narrative in 1 and 2 Peter. See also Abson Prédestin Joseph, *A Narratological Reading of 1 Peter* (London: Bloomsbury, 2013).

17 Green ("Narrating the Gospel," 274) explains the link between narrative and history as having a cognitive function ("the only true categories for making sense of daily existence are determined by . . . the scriptural story") and a formative one ("in selecting these particular events and in ordering them in this particular way, Peter is set on constructing the identity of the communities to which he has addressed himself").

18 Joel B. Green, *1 Peter* (Grand Rapids: Eerdmans, 2007), 22–23.

19 J. Ramsey Michaels (*1 Peter* [Waco, Tex.: Word, 1988], 17–18) suggests that the most closely related term to ἀναγεννήσας in Greek would be τὸν γεννήσαντα ("the parent," or "the one who begot"; cf. 1 John 5:1; Deuteronomy 32:18 LXX).

20 Cf. Green, *1 Peter*, 27–28.

21 Rather than recounting the history of the debate about the genre of 1 Peter (see the excellent summary in John H. Elliott, *1 Peter* [New York: Doubleday, 2001], 7–9), suffice it to say that the letter's massive section on ethical concerns (2:13–5:12) has occasioned J. de Waal Dryden's treatment from the perspective of virtue ethics and classified it as Greek paraenetic literature (*Theology and Ethics in 1 Peter: Paraenetic Strategies for Christian Character Formation* [Tübingen: Mohr Siebeck, 2006]). Dryden's repeated focus on Peter's ethical commands as inculcating a "*mind-set*" that changes attitudes by circumscribing an "internal reality that is to shape concrete action" (157; emphasis in original) is helpful to a point, but, as we will see it, fails to take into account the external *theological* reality that makes any internal change possible. Dryden is well aware of the change brought on by conversion. Indeed, he even notes that "identity breeds difference" (120) while discussing the election of the church, but this talk is left behind when addressing ethical injunctions themselves.

22 A number of recent works have dealt with Christian alterity in the New Testament, arguing that said rhetoric itself aids Peter and his audience to construct identity over and against the pagan culture. See especially Benjamin Dunning, *Aliens and Sojourners: Self as Other in Early Christianity* (Philadelphia: University of Pennsylvania Press, 2009); John H. Elliott, *A Home for the Homeless: A Social-Scientific Criticism of 1 Peter, Its Situation and Strategy* (Eugene, Ore.: Wipf & Stock, 2005).

23 Cf. Elliott, *1 Peter*, 81.

24 Green (*1 Peter*, 36–42) offers an existential reading of "the end of the ages" (1:20) that takes into account the experience of the revelation of Jesus Christ in the life of Peter's audience.

25 Reinhard Feldmeier's excursus on rebirth in his *First Letter of Peter* (129) points out that whatever salvation the new birth effects, it "is only present insofar as God's future in the form of hope already conditions the present of the believers." Elsewhere, Feldmeier ("Wiedergeburt im 1 Petrusbrief," in *Wiedergeburt* [ed. Reinhard Feldmeier; Göttingen: Vandenhoeck & Ruprecht, 2005], 86) notes that the experience of suffering "is deepened in light of the position of human beings between the eternal God and the 'empty' and perishing reality" (my translation).

26 It may be the case that the present argument inveighs against views that present 1 Peter as predicting an imminent apocalypse. That is, it was once common to suppose that Peter expects the eschaton to arrive shortly; he is authorizing a stopgap ethic by which to live in the interim. See, e.g., Leslie Kline, "Ethics for the End Time: An Exegesis of 1 Peter 4:7-11," *ResQ* 7 (1963): 11–23; Peter H. Davids, *The First Epistle of Peter* (Grand Rapids: Eerdmans, 1990), 155–56.

27 As we have argued above (ch. 4), early Christian thinking about birth from God indicates something like possession of God's DNA in the believer. This translates to a particular kind of character that is, as it were, natural, as in, "inherited" by the Christian from her parents. Something of the same logic operates in Petrine thinking about new birth.

28 Jürgen Moltmann, *The Spirit of Life: A Universal Affirmation* (trans. Margaret Kohl; Minneapolis: Fortress, 2001), 306.

29 Yves Congar, *I Believe in the Holy Spirit* (vol. 3; trans. Geoffrey Chapman; New York: Cassell, 1983), 213; quoted in Edward Siecienski, *The Filioque: History of a Doctrinal Controversy* (Oxford: Oxford University Press, 2010), 203.

30 Siecienski, *Filioque*, 203.

31 Jürgen Moltmann, *Trinity and the Kingdom* (trans. Margaret Kohl; Minneapolis: Fortress, 1993), 181.

32 Moltmann, *Spirit of Life*, 307.

33 Moltmann, *Trinity and the Kingdom*, 184.

34 Barth, *CD* II/2, 104. On this doctrine, see also Bruce McCormack, "Grace and Being: The Role of God's Gracious Election in Karl Barth's Theological Ontology," in *The Cambridge Companion to Karl Barth* (ed. John Webster; Cambridge: Cambridge University Press, 2000), who argues that Barth is quite serious about the divine election being an election of Jesus as subject from eternity. See a review of rejoinders to McCormack's view in James J. Cassady's "Election and Trinity," *WTJ* 71 (2009): 53–81. Also, see George Hunsinger's caution in "Election and the Trinity: Twenty-Five Theses on the Theology of Karl Barth," *MT* 24 (2008): 180. Without diving too deeply into the Barthian pool, we can at least say that God anticipates—the tensed verb

does not, of course, do justice—from eternity that the divine economy will be "cruciform" and "Jesus like."

35 Siecienski, *Filioque*, 73.

36 Interestingly, Gregory thinks of the Son as occupying the "middle position" or "mediation" (μεσιτείας, PG 45:133) so as to be the Only Begotten of the Father without negating the Father's originating the Spirit. It is not hard to see how this might express itself economically in a chronological placement. The first position (sender, originator) is held by the Father, the last place (life-giver) is held by the Spirit, and the middle position (the crucified one) is held by Christ. Notice also how the Spirit's life-giving presupposes the Son as being begotten and sent by the Father. In this way the Son's economic mission results in the Spirit's vivifying him in resurrection.

BIBLIOGRAPHY

Alexander, Neil. *The Epistles of John: Introduction and Commentary.* London: SCM Press, 1962.

Anderson, Paul N. "Gradations of Symbolization in the Johannine Passion Narrative." Pages 157–94 in *Imagery in the Gospel of John: Terms, Forms, Themes, and Theology of Johannine Figurative Language.* Edited by Jörg Frey, Jan G. van der Watt, Ruben Zimmerman, and Gabi Kern. Tübingen: Mohr Siebeck, 2006.

Anselm. *Prayers and Meditations of St. Anselm with the Proslogion.* Translated by Benedicta Ward. New York: Penguin, 1973.

Ansermet, François, and Pierre Magistretti. *Biology of Freedom: Neural Plasticity, Experience, and the Unconscious.* Translated by Susan Fairfield. London: Karnac, 2007.

Aristotle. *The "Art" of Rhetoric.* Translated by John Henky Freese. Loeb Classical Library. London: William Heinemann, 1926.

———. *Poetics.* Translated by D. W. Lucas. Oxford: Clarendon, 1968.

Athanasius. *St. Athanasius on the Incarnation: The Treatise de incarnatione verbi Dei.* Rev. ed. London: A.R. Mowbray, 1963.

Auerbach, Erich. *Mimesis.* Princeton: Princeton University Press, 1968.

Aulén, Gustaf. *Christus Victor: An Historical Study of the Three Main Types of the Idea of Atonement.* Translated by A. G. Herbert. New York: Macmillan, 1931.

Ayer, A. J. *Language, Truth, and Logic.* London: Victor Gallancz, 1936.

Baillet, Maurice. "Un Recueil Liturgique de Qumran, Grotte 4: 'Les Paroles des Luminaires.'" *Revue Biblique* 68 (1961): 195–250.

Baker, Mark D., and Joel B. Green. *Recovering the Scandal of the Cross: Atonement in New Testament and Contemporary Contexts*. 2nd ed. Downers Grove, Ill.: InterVarsity, 2011.

Baltzer, Klaus. *Deutero Isaiah*. Hermeneia. Minneapolis: Augsburg, 2001.

Barbour, Ian. *Myths, Models, and Paradigms: A Comparative Study in Science and Religion*. New York: Harper & Row, 1974.

Barth, Karl. *Church Dogmatics*. Translated by G. W. Bromiley, G. T. Thompson, and Harold Knight. 13 vols. London: T&T Clark, 2010.

Bauks, Michaela. "The Theological Implications of Child Sacrifice in and beyond the Biblical Context in Relation to Genesis 22 and Judges II." Pages 65–86 in *Human Sacrifice in Jewish and Christian Tradition*. Edited by K. Finsterbusch, A. Lange, and K. F. D. Römheld. Leiden: Brill, 2007.

Baumann, Gerd. *The Multicultural Riddle: Rethinking National, Ethnic, and Religious Identities*. London: Routledge, 1999.

Biddle, Mark E. *Missing the Mark: Sin and Its Consequences in Biblical Theology*. Nashville: Abingdon, 2005.

Black, Max. "Metaphor." *Proceedings of the Aristotelian Society* 55 (1954): 273–94.

———. *Models and Metaphors*. Ithaca, N.Y.: Cornell University Press, 1962.

Bock, Darrell. *Acts*. Grand Rapids: Baker, 2007.

Boda, Mark J. *A Severe Mercy: Sin and Its Remedy in the Old Testament*. Winona Lake, Ind.: Eisenbrauns, 2009.

Boersma, Hans. *Violence, Hospitality, and the Cross: Reappropriating the Atonement Tradition*. Grand Rapids: Baker Academic, 2004.

Bonhoeffer, Dietrich. *Ethics*. Translated by Neville Horton Smith. New York: Macmillan, 1955.

Boyd, Richard. "Metaphor and Theory Change." Pages 356–408 in *Metaphor and Thought*. Edited by Andrew Ortony. Cambridge: Cambridge University Press, 1979.

Brown, Raymond E. *The Epistles of John: Translated with Introduction, Notes, and Commentary*. New York: Doubleday, 1982.

———. *The Gospel According to John*. 2 vols. Garden City, N.Y.: Doubleday, 1970.

Bruner, Frederick Dale. *The Gospel of John: A Commentary*. Grand Rapids: Eerdmans, 2012.

Bynum, Caroline Walker. *Fragmentation and Redemption: Essays on Gender and the Human Body in Medieval Religion*. New York: Zone Books, 1991.

———. *Jesus as Mother: Studies in the Spirituality of the High Middle Ages*. Berkeley: University of California Press, 1982.

Cassady, James J. "Election and Trinity." *Westminster Theological Journal* 71 (2009): 53–81.

Castelo, Daniel. *The Apathetic God: Exploring the Contemporary Relevance of Divine Impassibility*. Eugene, Ore.: Wipf & Stock, 2009.

Childs, Brevard. *Isaiah: A Commentary*. Louisville, Ky.: Westminster John Knox, 2001.

Christensen, Duane. *Deuteronomy 21:10–34:12*. Nashville: Nelson, 2002.

Clement of Alexandria. *Paedagogus*. Translated by G. W. Butterworth. Loeb Classical Library. Cambridge: Harvard University Press, 1919.

Cockerill, Gareth Lee. *The Epistle to the Hebrews*. Grand Rapids: Eerdmans, 2012.

Congar, Yves. *I Believe in the Holy Spirit*. Vol. 3. Translated by Geoffrey Chapman. New York: Cassell, 1983.

Craigie, Peter C. *The Book of Deuteronomy*. Grand Rapids: Eerdmans, 1976.

Crysdale, Cynthia. S. W. *Embracing Travail*. New York: Continuum, 2001.

Cullinan, Colleen Carpenter. "In Pain and Sorrow: Childbirth, Incarnation, and the Suffering of Women." *Cross Currents* 58 (2008): 95–107.

Darr, Kathryn Pfisterrer. "Like Warrior, Like Woman: Destruction and Deliverance in Isaiah 42:10-17." *Catholic Biblical Quarterly* 49 (1987): 560–71.

———. "Two Unifying Female Images in the Book of Isaiah." Pages 17–30 in *Uncovering Ancient Stones: Essays in Memory of H. Neil Richardson*. Edited by L. M. Hopfe. Winona Lake, Ind.: Eisenbrauns, 1994.

Davids, Peter H. *The First Epistle of Peter*. Grand Rapids: Eerdmans, 1990.

Derrida, Jacques. *The Gift of Death*. Translated by David Wills. Chicago: University of Chicago Press, 1995.

———. *Given Time: I. Counterfeit Money*. Translated by Peggy Kamuf. Chicago: University of Chicago Press, 1992.

———. "On the Gift: A Discussion between Jacques Derrida and Jean-Luc Marion." Pages 54–78 in *God, the Gift, and Postmodernism*. Edited by John D. Caputo and Michael J. Scanlon. Bloomington: Indiana University Press, 1999.

deSilva, David. *Honor, Patronage, Kinship, and Purity: Unlocking New Testament Culture*. Downers Grove, Ill.: IVP Academic, 2000.

Dodd, Charles H. *Johannine Epistles*. London: Harper & Row, 1946.

Dryden, J. de Waal. "The Sense of σπέρμα in 1 John 3:9 in Light of the Lexical Evidence." *Estudios de Filología Neotestamentaria* 11 (1998): 85–100.

———. *Theology and Ethics in 1 Peter: Paraenetic Strategies for Christian Character Formation.* Tübingen: Mohr Siebeck, 2006.

Dryden, John. *The Works of John Dryden.* Vol. 8. Berkeley: University of California Press, 1965.

Dunn, James D. G. *Romans 1–8.* Dallas: Word, 1988.

Dunning, Benjamin. *Aliens and Sojourners: Self as Other in Early Christianity.* Philadelphia: University of Pennsylvania Press, 2009.

Eckart, Otto. "Moses Abschiedslied in Deuteronomium 32: Ein Zeugnis der Kanonsbildung in der Hebräischen Bibel." Pages 641–78 in *Die Tora.* Wiesbaden: Harrassowitz, 2009.

Elliott, John H. *1 Peter.* New York: Doubleday, 2001.

———. *A Home for the Homeless: A Social-Scientific Criticism of 1 Peter, Its Situation and Strategy.* Eugene, Ore.: Wipf & Stock, 2005.

Engberg-Pedersen, Troels. "Gift-Giving and Friendship: Seneca and Paul in Romans 1–8 on the Logic of God's χάρις and Its Human Response." *Harvard Theological Review* 101 (2008): 15–44.

Faraday, Michael. "10 November, 1845." Page 331 in *Diary.* Vol. 4. London: G. Bell & Sons, 1933.

Feldmeier, Reinhard. *The First Letter of Peter: A Commentary on the Greek Text.* Translated by Peter H. Davids. Waco, Tex.: Baylor University Press, 2008.

———. "Wiedergeburt im 1 Petrusbrief." Pages 75–99 in *Wiedergeburt.* Edited by Reinhard Feldmeier. Göttingen: Vandenhoeck & Ruprecht, 2005.

Ferré, Frederick. *Language, Logic, and God.* London: Eyre & Spottiswoode, 1962.

Feuillet, André. "L'heure de la femme (Jn 16,21) et l'heure de la Mére de Jésus (Jn 19,25-27)." *Biblica* 47 (1966): 169–84.

Fiddes, Paul S. *The Creative Suffering of God.* Oxford: Clarendon, 1992.

Finlan, Stephen. *Problems with Atonement.* Collegeville, Minn.: Liturgical, 2005.

Ford, J. Massyngbaerde. *Redeemer, Friend, and Mother: Salvation in Antiquity and in the Gospel of John.* Minneapolis: Fortress, 1997.

Foster, Julia A. "The Use of ḥyl as God-Language in the Hebrew Scriptures." Pages 93–102 in *Uncovering Ancient Stones: Essays in Memory of H. Neil Richardson.* Edited by Lewis M. Hopfe. Winona Lake, Ind.: Eisenbrauns, 1994.

Frei, Hans. *The Eclipse of Biblical Narrative: A Study in Eighteenth and Nineteenth Century Hermeneutics*. New Haven: Yale University Press, 1974.

Gaventa, Beverly Roberts. "The Cosmic Power of Sin in Paul's Letter to the Romans: Toward a Widescreen Edition." *Interpretation* 58 (2004): 229–40.

———. *From Darkness to Light: Aspects of Conversion in the New Testament*. Minneapolis: Fortress, 1986.

Girard, René. *I See Satan Fall like Lightning*. Translated by James G. Williams. Maryknoll, N.Y.: Orbis, 2001.

———. *Violence and the Sacred*. Translated by Patrick Gregory. Baltimore: Johns Hopkins University Press, 1977. English translation of *La Violence et le sacré*. Paris: Editions Bernard Grasset, 1972.

Goldingay, John. *After Eating the Apricot*. Carlisle, UK: Paternoster, 1996.

———. *Psalms 90–150*. Grand Rapids: Baker Academic, 2008.

Goldingay, John, and David Payne. *A Critical and Exegetical Commentary on Isaiah 40–55*. Vol. 1. New York: T&T Clark, 2006.

González, Justo L. *Luke*. Louisville, Ky.: Westminster John Knox, 2010.

Gorman, Michael J. *Cruciformity: Paul's Narrative Spirituality of the Cross*. Grand Rapids: Eerdmans, 2001.

Green, Joel B. *1 Peter*. Grand Rapids: Eerdmans, 2007.

———. *Body, Soul, and Human Life: The Nature of Humanity in the Bible*. Grand Rapids: Baker Academic, 2008.

———. *The Gospel of Luke*. Grand Rapids: Eerdmans, 1997.

———. "Narrating the Gospel in 1 and 2 Peter." *Interpretation* 60 (2006): 262–77.

Greese, William. "'Unless One Is Born Again': The Use of a Heavenly Journey in John 3." *Journal of Biblical Literature* 107 (1988): 677–93.

Gregory, Chris. *Gifts and Commodities*. London: Academic Press, 1982.

Gregory of Nazianzus. "Letters on the Apollinarian Controversy" (Ep. 101). Pages 215–32 in *Christology of the Later Fathers*. Edited by Edward R. Hardy. Translated by Charles Gordon Brown and James Edward Swallow. Louisville, Ky.: Westminster John Knox, 1954.

Grohmann, Marianne. "Metaphors of God, Nature and Birth." Pages 23–33 in *Metaphors in the Psalms*. Edited by Pierre van Hecke and Antje Labahn. Leuven: Uitgeverij Peeters, 2010.

Gruber, Meyer. "The Motherhood of God in Second Isaiah." *Revue Biblique* 90 (1983): 351–59.

Gunton, Colin. *The Actuality of the Atonement: A Study of Metaphor, Rationality, and the Christian Tradition*. London: T&T Clark, 1988.

————. *A Brief Theology of Revelation*. London: T&T Clark, 1995.

Heim, Mark S. *Saved from Sacrifice: A Theology of the Cross*. Grand Rapids: Eerdmans, 2006.

Hengel, Martin. *Crucifixion*. Translated by John Bowden. Philadelphia: Fortress, 1977.

Hesse, Mary. *Models and Analogies in Science*. Notre Dame, Ind.: Notre Dame University Press, 1966.

Hill, Charles. "Atonement in the Apocalypse of John: 'A Lamb Standing as if Slain.'" Pages 190–207 in *The Glory of the Atonement: Biblical, Historical, and Practical Perspectives*. Edited by Charles Hill and Frank James. Downers Grove, Ill.: InterVarsity, 2004.

Hill, John Spencer. "τὰ βαΐα τῶν φοινίκων [John 12:13]: Pleonasm or Prolepsis?" *Journal of Biblical Literature* 101 (1982): 133–35.

Himbaza, I. "Dt 32, 8, une Correction Tardive des Scribes: Essai D'interprétation et de Datation." *Biblica* 83 (2002): 527–48.

Hodge, Caroline Johnson. *If Sons, Then Heirs: A Study of Kinship and Ethnicity in the Letters of Paul*. Oxford: Oxford University Press, 2007.

Hunsinger, George. "Election and the Trinity: Twenty-Five Theses on the Theology of Karl Barth." *Modern Theology* 24 (2008): 179–98.

————. *How to Read Karl Barth: The Shape of His Theology*. Oxford: Oxford University Press, 1991.

Jenson, Robert W. *Canon and Creed*. Louisville, Ky.: Westminster John Knox, 2010.

Jobes, Karen H. *1 Peter*. Grand Rapids: Baker Academic, 2005.

Johnson, Elizabeth A. *She Who Is: The Mystery of God in Feminist Theological Discourse*. New York: Crossroad, 1994.

Joosten, Jan. "A Note on the Text of Deuteronomy xxxii 8." *Vetus Testamentum* 57 (2007): 548–55.

Joseph, Abson Prédestin. *A Narratological Reading of 1 Peter*. London: Bloomsbury, 2013.

Julian of Norwich. *Showings*. Edited and translated by Edmund Colledge and James Walsh. Mahwah, N.J.: Paulist, 1978.

Jüngel, Eberhard. *God as the Mystery of the World: On the Foundation of the Theology of the Crucified One in the Dispute between Theism and Atheism*. Translated by Darrell L. Guder. Grand Rapids: Eerdmans, 1983.

Käsemann, Ernst. "Titus 3:4-7." Pages 298–302 in *Exegetische Versuche und Besinnungen I*. Göttingen: Vandenhoeck & Ruprecht, 1965.

Keiser, Thomas A. "The Song of Moses a Basis for Isaiah's Prophecy." *Vetus Testamentum* 55 (2005): 486–500.

Kim, Hyun Chul Paul. "The Song of Moses (Deuteronomy 32:1-43) in Isaiah 40–55." Pages 147–71 in *God's Word for Our World: Biblical Studies in Honor of Simon John De Vries*. Vol. 1. Edited by J. H. Ellens, D. I. Ellens, R. P. Knierem, and I. Kalimi. New York: T&T Clark, 2004.

Kline, Leslie. "Ethics for the End Time: An Exegesis of 1 Peter 4:7-11." *Restoration Quarterly* 7 (1963): 11–23.

Knierim, Rolf. *Die Hauptbegriffe fuer Suende im Alten Testament*. Gütersloh: Mohn, 1965.

Knight, Douglas. "From Metaphor to Mediation: Colin Gunton and the Concept of Mediation." *Neue Zeitschrift für Systematische Theologie und Religionsphilosophie* 43 (2001): 118–36.

Köckert, Matthias. "Zeit und Ewigkeit in Psalm 90." Pages 155–85 in *Zeit und Ewigkeit als Raum göttlichen Handelns: Religionsgeschichtliche, theologische und philosophische Perspektiven*. Edited by Reinhard G. Kratz and Hermann Spieckermann. Berlin: de Gruyter, 2009.

Kraus, Hans-Joachim. *Psalms 60–150: A Commentary*. Minneapolis: Augsburg, 1989.

Kruse, Colin. *The Letters of John*. Grand Rapids: Eerdmans, 2000.

———. *Paul's Letter to the Romans*. Grand Rapids: Eerdmans, 2012.

Kuhn, Thomas. *The Structure of Scientific Revolutions*. Chicago: University of Chicago Press, 1962.

Laidlaw, James. "A Free Gift Makes No Friends." Pages 45–66 in *The Question of the Gift: Essays across Disciplines*. Edited by Mark Osteen. New York: Routledge, 2002.

Lakatos, Imre. *Proofs and Refutations: The Logic of Mathematical Discovery*. Cambridge: Cambridge University Press, 1976.

Leuchter, Mark. "Why Is the Song of Moses in the Book of Deuteronomy?" *Vetus Testamentum* 57 (2007): 295–317.

Levinson, Jon D. *Creation and the Persistence of Evil: The Jewish Drama of Divine Omnipotence*. Princeton: Princeton University Press, 1988.

Lewis, C. S. *A Grief Observed*. London: Faber, 1961.

Lindbeck, George. *The Nature of Doctrine: Religion and Theology in a Postliberal Age*. Louisville, Ky.: Westminster John Knox, 1984.

Loewe, William P. "Encountering the Crucified God: The Soteriology of Sebastian Moore." *Horizons* 2 (1982): 216–36.

———. "Irenaeus' Soteriology: *Christus Victor* Revisited." *Anglican Theological Review* 67 (1985): 1–15.

Mahony, John W. "A Theology of Sin for Today." Pages 187–217 in *Fallen: A Theology of Sin*. Edited by Christopher W. Morgan and Robert A. Peterson. Wheaton, Ill.: Crossway, 2013.

Manns, Frédéric. "La Théologie de la Nouvelle Naissance dans la Première Lettre de Pierre." *Liber Annus* 45 (1995): 107–41.

Marguerite D'Oingt. *The Writings of Margaret of Oingt, Medieval Prioress and Mystic (d. 1310)*. Edited and translated by Renate Blumenfeld-Kosinski. Newburyport, Mass.: Focus Information Group, 1990.

Markham, Paul. *Rewired: Exploring Religious Conversion*. Eugene, Ore.: Wipf & Stock, 2007.

Marsh, John. *Saint John*. Harmondsworth: Penguin, 1968.

Matson, Mark. *In Dialogue with Another Gospel? The Influence of the Fourth Gospel on the Passion Narrative of the Gospel of Luke*. Atlanta: SBL, 2001.

McClendon, James Wm., Jr., and James M. Smith. "Ian Ramsey's Model of Religious Language: A Qualified Appreciation." *Journal of the American Academy of Religion* 41 (1973): 413–24.

McConville, J. Gordon. *Being Human in God's World: An Old Testament Theology of Humanity*. Grand Rapids: Baker Academic, 2016.

McCormack, Bruce. "Grace and Being: The Role of God's Gracious Election in Karl Barth's Theological Ontology." Pages 92–110 in *The Cambridge Companion to Karl Barth*. Edited by John Webster. Cambridge: Cambridge University Press, 2000.

McFarland, Ian A. *In Adam's Fall: A Meditation on the Christian Doctrine of Original Sin*. West Sussex: Wiley-Blackwell, 2010.

McGinn, Colin. *Basic Structures of Reality: Essays on Meta-physics*. Oxford: Oxford University Press, 2011.

McKnight, Scot. *A Community Called Atonement*. Nashville: Abingdon, 2007.

Michaels, J. Ramsey. *1 Peter*. Waco, Tex.: Word, 1988.

———. *The Gospel of John*. Grand Rapids: Eerdmans, 2010.

———. *John*. Grand Rapids: Baker, 1984.

Middleton, J. Richard. *The Liberating Image: The* Imago Dei *in Genesis 1*. Grand Rapids: Brazos, 2005.

Milbank, John. "'I Will Gasp and Pant': Deutero-Isaiah and the Birth of the Suffering Subject." *Semeia* 59 (1992): 59–71.

Miller, Patrick D. *Interpreting the Psalms*. Philadelphia: Fortress, 1986.

Mitchell, Basil. *Faith and Logic: Oxford Essays in Philosophical Theology*. Boston: Beacon, 1957.

Moberly, R. W. L. "Did the Serpent Get It Right?" *Journal of Theological Studies* 39 (1988): 1–27.

Moltmann, Jürgen. *The Crucified God*. Translated by R. A. Wilson and John Bowden. Minneapolis: Fortress, 1993.

————. *God in Creation: A New Theology of Creation and the Spirit of God*. Translated by Margaret Kohl. Minneapolis: Fortress, 1993.

————. *The Spirit of Life: A Universal Affirmation*. Translated by Margaret Kohl. Minneapolis: Fortress, 2001.

————. *Trinity and the Kingdom*. Translated by Margaret Kohl. Minneapolis: Fortress, 1993.

Moo, Douglas. *Epistle to the Roman*. Grand Rapids: Eerdmans, 1996.

————. "Sin in Paul." Pages 107–30 in *Fallen: A Theology of Sin*. Edited by Christopher W. Morgan and Robert A. Peterson. Wheaton, Ill.: Crossway, 2013.

Morgan, Jonathan. "*Christus Victor* Motifs in the Soteriology of Thomas Aquinas." *Pro Ecclesia* 21 (2012): 409–21.

Morris, Leon. *The Gospel According to John*. Grand Rapids: Eerdmans, 1995.

Muilenburg, James. "The Book of Isaiah: Chapters 40–66." Pages 381–773 in vol. 5 of *The Interpreter's Bible*. Nashville: Abingdon, 1956.

Muis, J. "The Truth of Metaphorical God-Talk." *Scottish Journal of Theology* 63 (2010): 146–62.

Murphy, Nancey. *Bodies and Souls, or Spirited Bodies?* Cambridge: Cambridge University Press, 2006.

Nietzsche, Friedrich. *Genealogy of Morals*. Translated by Carol Diethe. Cambridge: Cambridge University Press, 1994.

Noort, Edward. "Human Sacrifice and Theology in the Hebrew Bible." Pages 1–20 in *The Sacrifice of Isaac: The Aqedah and Its Interpretation*. Edited by E. Noort and E. J. C. Tigchelaar. Leiden: Brill, 2002.

Nozick, Robert. "Coercion." Pages 440–72 in *Philosophy, Science, and Method: Essays in Honor of Ernest Nagel*. Edited by S. Morgenbesser, P. Suppes, and M. White. New York: St. Martin's, 1969.

Okure, Teresa. "The Significance Today of Jesus's Commission to Mary Magdalene." *International Review of Mission* 81 (1992): 177–88.

Oldenhage, Tania. "Jesus' Labor Pain: Rereading Birth and Crisis in the Passion Narratives." *Lectio Difficilior* 2 (2012). Available online at http://www.lectio.unibe.ch/12_2/oldenhage_tania_jesus_labor_pain.html.

Orr, William, and William Guy. *Living Hope: A Study of the New Testament Theme of Birth from Above*. Santa Fe, N.M.: Sunstone Press, 1989.

Oswalt, John. *The Book of Isaiah 40–66*. Grand Rapids: Eerdmans, 1998.

Painter, John. "The 'Opponents' in 1 John." *New Testament Studies* 32 (1986): 48–71.

Pannenberg, Wolfhart. "The Doctrine of Creation and Modern Science." Pages 29–49 in *Toward a Theology of Nature: Essays on Science and Faith*. Edited by Wolfhart Pannenberg and Ted Peters. Louisville, Ky.: Westminster John Knox, 1993.

Patrologia graeca. Edited by J.-P. Migne. 162 vols. Paris, 1857–1886.

Pentz, Rebecca D. "Can Jesus Save Women?" Pages 77–110 in *Encountering Jesus: A Debate on Christology*. Edited by Stephen T. Davis. Atlanta: John Knox, 1988.

Peterson, David G. *The Acts of the Apostles*. Grand Rapids: Eerdmans, 2009.

Philo. *On the Sacrifices of Cain and Abel*. Translated by F. H. Colson. Loeb Classical Library. Cambridge, Mass.: Harvard University Press, 1929.

———. *On the Special Laws*. Translated by F. H. Colson. Loeb Classical Library. Cambridge, Mass.: Harvard University Press, 1937.

Polanyi, Michael. *Personal Knowledge: Towards a Post-critical Philosophy*. London: Routledge, 1958.

Popper, Karl. *The Logic of Scientific Discovery*. London: Hutchinson, 1952.

Rae, Murray. "The Travail of God." *International Journal of Systematic Theology* 5 (2003): 47–61.

Ramsey, Ian. *Models and Mystery*. Oxford: Oxford University Press, 1964.

———. *Religious Language: An Empirical Placing of Theological Phrases*. New York: Macmillan, 1957.

Richards, I. A. *The Philosophy of Rhetoric*. Oxford: Oxford University Press, 1936.

Ricoeur, Paul. *The Conflict of Interpretations: Essays in Hermeneutics*. Edited by Don Ihde. Evanston, Ill.: Northwestern University Press, 1974.

———. *The Rule of Metaphor: Multidisciplinary Studies in the Creation of Meaning in Language*. Translated by Robert Czerny. New York: Routledge, 2003.

Rizzolatti, Giacomo, and Maddalena Fabbri-Destro. "The Mirror Mechanism: Understanding Others from the Inside." Pages 264–90 in *Understanding Other Minds: Perspectives from Developmental*

Social Neuroscience. Edited by Simon Baron-Cohen, Helen Tager-Flusberg, and Michael V. Lombardo. Oxford: Oxford University Press, 2013.

Röhl, Johannes. "Ontological Categories for Fields and Waves." *Lecture Notes in Informatics* (2013): 1866–74.

Russell, Bertrand, and Alfred North Whitehead. *Principia Mathematica*. Vol. 1. Cambridge: Cambridge University Press, 1910.

Sanders, Paul. *The Provenance of Deuteronomy 32*. Leiden: Brill, 1996.

Schaefer, Konrad. *Psalms*. Collegeville, Minn.: Liturgical, 2001.

Schmiechen, Peter. *Saving Power: Theories of Atonement and Forms of the Church*. Grand Rapids: Eerdmans, 2005.

Schnackenburg, Rudolph. *The Johannine Epistles*. New York: Crossroad, 1992.

Siecienski, Edward. *The Filioque: History of a Doctrinal Controversy*. Oxford: Oxford University Press, 2010.

Skehan, Patrick W. "The Structure of the Song of Moses in Deuteronomy [Dt 32:1-43]." *Catholic Biblical Quarterly* 13 (1951): 153–63.

Soskice, Janet Martin. *Metaphor and Religious Language*. Oxford: Clarendon, 1985.

Stibbe, Mark W. G. *John*. Sheffield: JSOT Press, 1993.

Stiver, Dan. *Theology after Ricoeur: New Directions in Hermeneutical Theology*. Louisville, Ky.: Westminster John Knox, 2001.

Streufert, Mary. "Maternal Sacrifice as a Hermeneutics of the Cross." Pages 63–75 in *Cross Examinations: Readings on the Meaning of the Cross Today*. Edited by Merit Trelstad. Minneapolis: Augsburg Fortress, 2006.

Stuhlmacher, Peter. *Paul's Letter to the Romans: A Commentary*. Louisville, Ky.: Westminster John Knox, 1994.

Sunstein, Cass R., and Richard H. Thaler. *Nudge: Improving Decisions about Health, Wealth, and Happiness*. New Haven: Yale University Press, 2008.

Szwarc, Urszula. "Skała Izraela w Świetle Wiersza Pwt 32, 18." *Roczniki Teologiczne* 49 (2002): 5–13.

Talbert, Charles. *Reading John: A Literary and Theological Commentary on the Fourth Gospel and the Johannine Epistles*. New York: Crossroad, 1992.

Tannehill, Robert C. *Dying and Rising with Christ: A Study in Pauline Theology*. Berlin: Alfred Töpelmann, 1966.

Tate, Marvin. *Psalms 51–100*. Dallas: Word, 1990.

Theissen, Gerd. *The Miracle Stories of the Early Christian Tradition.* Translated by Francis McDonagh. Minneapolis: Fortress, 1982.

Tilley, Terrence. "Ian Ramsey and Empirical Fit." *Journal of the American Academy of Religion* 45 (1977): 963–88.

Towner, Philip. *The Letters to Timothy and Titus.* Grand Rapids: Eerdmans, 2006.

Trible, Phyllis. *God and the Rhetoric of Sexuality.* Philadelphia: Fortress, 1978.

Trudinger, Paul. "An Autobiographical Digression? A Note on Romans 7:7-25." *Expository Times* 107 (1996): 173–74.

van Driel, Edwin Chr. "Karl Barth and the Eternal Existence of Jesus Christ." *Scottish Journal of Theology* 60 (2007): 45–61.

Vanhoozer, Kevin. "The Atonement in Postmodernity: Guilt, Goats, and Gifts." Pages 367–403 in *The Glory of the Atonement: Biblical, Historical, and Practical Perspectives.* Edited by Charles E. Hill and Frank A. James III. Downers Grove, Ill.: InterVarsity, 2004.

Watts, John D. W. *Isaiah 1–33.* Waco, Tex.: Word, 1985.

———. *Isaiah 34–66.* Waco, Tex.: Word, 1987.

Weaver, J. Denny. *The Nonviolent Atonement.* Grand Rapids: Eerdmans, 2001.

Webb, Barry. "Zion in Transformation: A Literary Approach to Isaiah." Pages 65–84 in *The Bible in Three Dimensions: Essays in Honor of Forty Years of Biblical Studies in the University of Sheffield.* Edited by D. J. A. Clines et al. Sheffield: JSOT Press, 1992.

Weinandy, Thomas G. *Does God Suffer?* Notre Dame, Ind.: University of Notre Dame Press, 2000.

Westermann, Claus. *Isaiah 40–66.* London: SCM Press, 1969.

Wilson-Kastner, Patricia. *Faith, Feminism, and the Christ.* Philadelphia: Fortress, 1983.

Wink, Walter. *Engaging the Powers: Discernment and Resistance in a World of Domination.* Minneapolis: Fortress, 1992.

Witherington, Ben, III. *The Acts of the Apostles: A Socio-rhetorical Commentary.* Grand Rapids: Eerdmans, 1997.

Wright, N. T. *Paul and the Faithfulness of God.* Minneapolis: Fortress, 2013.

———. "Romans." Pages 562–72 in *The New Interpreter's Bible: Acts–1 Corinthians.* Edited by Leander Keck. Nashville: Abingdon, 2002.

Yarbrough, Robert. *1–3 John.* Grand Rapids: Baker Academic, 2008.

Young, Josiah. "Dietrich Bonhoeffer and Reinhold Niebuhr: Their Ethics, Views on Karl Barth, and Perspectives on African Americans." Pages 283–300 in *Bonhoeffer's Intellectual Formation: Theology and Philosophy in His Thought*. Edited by Peter Frick. Tübingen: Mohr Siebeck, 2008.

Zimmerman, Christiane. "Wiederentstehung und Erneuerung (Tit 3:5): Zu einem erhaltenswerten Aspekt der Soteriologie des Titusbriefs." *Novum Testamentum* 51 (2009): 272–95.

SCRIPTURE INDEX

Genesis
1:2	55, 56
1:4, 6, 9	56
3	65
3:16	57, 91

Exodus
15:3	48

Leviticus
10:1-2	66
12:7	63
15:30	63

Numbers
21:4-9	46

Deuteronomy
31:29	92
32:18 LXX	123n19
32:1-43	90–92, 122n8

Psalms
42:2	51
45:6-7	35
48:4-6	47
51	67
51:12-14	116n14
90	52–55, 114n41
90:2	53, 56, 91
104:28-30	70, 72

Proverbs
23:22	91

Isaiah
5:18-20	63
7:14	47
8:3	47
9:5-6	52
13:6-8	47
13:8	47
21:3	47
26:17	47
42:13-17	46–47, 52, 111n15
49:20	47
53	96

Jeremiah
1:7-10	66
6:24	48
30:5-6	48
49:24	48
50:43	48

Ezekiel
36:3	111n15
36:25	68
36:26-27	69
36:28	68
37:23	68

Hosea
  13:13   47, 112n23
Joel
  2:21-24   72
  2:28-29   71
Micah
  4:9-10   112n23
  5:2   47, 112n23
Mark
  12:27   51
Luke
  8:21   76
  23:34   42
  24:25-27   35
John
  1:12-14   74
  3:3-7   6, 27, 105n4
  3:5   7
  3:14   46
  3:14-16   46
  7:37-39   7–8
  8:28   46
  12:13   118n27
  12:32   46
  16:21   13, 39
  19:28-30   45–46
Acts
  5   66
Romans
  1–8   83, 120n14
  5–8   94
  5   83, 88
  5:5   93–94
  5:6-21   82
  5:12   65
  5:17   85
  6   81
  6:14   115n8
  7:8   116n12
  7:19   65, 115n8
  7:24-25   88
  8   93
  8:1-10   72
  8:11   93

  8:14-21   71
  9–11   93
  12:12   76
1 Corinthians
  13:9   20
2 Corinthians
  5:17   92
Galatians
  4:9   7
Ephesians
  2:11-22   121n25
Titus
  1   68
  2   68
  2:14   68
  3   67
  3:4-7   68, 70, 117n25
  3:5   6, 70, 117n25
  3:6   71
  3:7   71, 117n20
  3:8, 14   72
Hebrews
  1:8-9   35
  9:11-14   36
  12:2   48
James
  1:17   7
1 Peter
  1   96–98
  1:23   6, 98
  2:13, 16   97
  2:19-25   96
  3:1-2   97
  3:18   98
1 John
  2:14   73
  3   72
  3:9   72, 118n30
  3:10   73
  5:1   123n19
Revelation
  12:2   13

SUBJECT INDEX

Anselm, 9–12, 102
Aristotle, 30–34
Athanasius, 56

Barth, Karl, 57, 64, 84, 101, 114n47, 115n7, 124n34
Bible, 3, 11, 20, 35, 106n17, 108n9
blood, 11, 14, 27, 36; and water, 5, 9, 14, 76, 102
Bonhoeffer, Dietrich, 64, 115n7
born again, 6–7, 59, 103

canon, canonical form, 35–37, 47, 55–56, 108n9
Christus Victor, 4, 49, 77, 84, 119n5
coercion, 43–44, 56
conversion, 6, 45, 53, 58, 74–75, 123n21
covenant, covenantal, 68, 69, 85–88, 116n12
creation, 11–14, 37, 53–59, 70–72, 85, 89, 92–95, 100–101, 113n32, 114n47; and redemption, 13, 70, 72, 113n32; new, 86, 113n34
cross: offense, 1–2
Cur Deus Homo, 12

damage, 40, 63, 111n13
debt, 1, 12, 80–84, 121n26
demonic, 41–42, 48, 53, 58–59, 67
Derrida, Jacques, 81–82, 86, 88
DNA, 8, 62, 72–76, 118n31, 121n24, 124n27

ecclesiology, 67–68, 72, 74–76, 86, 89–90
economy, 4, 14, 29, 38, 57, 80–83, 86–88, 92, 95, 99–101, 125n34
election, 85, 89, 90–96, 100–103, 123n1; Christ as subject of, 57, 114n47, 124n34; of Israel, 13, 37, 89, 90–96, 100
eschatology, 20, 44, 69–71, 87, 96, 98–103, 121n24, 124n26
eternity, eternal, 9, 20, 46, 49–59, 68, 74, 82, 84, 96, 100–102, 113n31, 113n39, 114n47, 114n48, 124n25, 124n34
evil, 42, 49, 55, 57, 63–65, 97, 116n12, 119n5

feminist interpretation, 5, 12–13, 103
filioque, 99–102

gender, 28, 37, 103, 122n8
gift, giftedness, 77, 80–88, 94, 119n11, 120n14, 122n12; of the Spirit, 20, 37
Girard, René, 41–42, 44, 49, 88, 119n5
God-born, 27, 37, 58, 72–76, 80, 86, 103, 121n25
Godhead, 4, 51–52, 57, 89, 101, 114n47
God's being, 14, 57–59, 114n47, 114n48
grace, graciousness, 3, 5, 12, 64, 68, 80, 82–83, 85, 120n14
Gregory of Nyssa, 102, 125n36

hamartiology, 65–67, 85, 116n12
harm, 5, 40–45, 48, 58
honor, 12, 67, 79
humiliation, 1, 12, 41, 53
hypostasis, hypostases, 51, 93, 99–100

immanent, immanence, 57–58, 89, 99–102
impassibility, 14, 40, 49–54, 89, 112n29
incarnate, incarnation, 11–13, 49, 51–52, 80, 82, 92, 100–101, 113n32, 114n47
inheritance, 67, 71–72, 96–98, 121n25, 124n27

Julian of Norwich, 10–12, 102
Jüngel, Eberhard, 50–52
justice, justification, 61, 66, 68, 70, 77, 79, 86, 93, 117n20

labor metaphor, 9–15, 27, 32, 40, 45, 48, 52–56, 113n32
linguistic novelty, 23–24, 31
literary network, 20, 35–37
logical positivism, 18, 37

Marguerite d'Oingt, 10–12, 102
Maximus the Confessor, 102
Moltmann, Jürgen, 51, 70–71, 99–102

moral influence, 32, 61, 79–80, 119n5
Mother Jesus, 9–12, 14, 86, 92, 101–3

neural networks, 74–75
Nicodemus, 7, 46, 105n5
Nietzsche, Friedrich, 80–81, 83–84, 120n11
nonviolence, 43–45, 49, 56–58, 79, 119n5
Nozick, Robert, 43

objective models of atonement, 77, 79–80, 84–85
ontology, 22, 69, 72, 74–75, 87, 108n12, 108n15

penal substitution, 40, 42, 61–62, 77–80
philosophy of language, 18, 108n12
pneumatology, 14, 89, 92
poetry, poetic language, 8, 14, 28, 32–35, 47, 69, 90, 110n41
procession: divine, 14, 89, 99; of the Spirit, 38, 94, 100–102, 114n48

Rahner, Karl, 99, 100
ransom, 1, 3, 14, 32, 79–80
rebellion, rebellious, 91–92, 94, 118n30
religious metaphor, 19, 24, 32, 37, 120n19
Ricoeur, Paul, 30–35, 82–85, 109n29, 109n33, 109n35, 110n41, 120n17

sacrifice, 1–2, 4, 12–14, 24, 28–36, 41–42, 77–83, 87–88
salvation, 9–11, 56, 85, 95–99; of Israel, 100
satisfaction, 9–10, 20, 42, 62, 77, 80, 82
scapegoat, scapegoating, 28, 41–42, 48, 67, 78, 119n5
Soskice, Janet Martin, 25, 29, 31, 108n21

spiritual children, 9, 27, 37, 52, 72,
   74, 80, 88
subjective models of atonement,
   79–80
substitution, 12, 14, 20, 29, 78–80,
   83, 87
suffering, 9–10, 12, 39–58, 62, 67,
   93–98, 101, 113n31, 114n48

teologia crucis, 3–6, 50
Torah, 66–69, 79, 82, 115n8, 117n20,
   120n17
transformative, transformation, 34,
   39, 44–49, 58, 66–69, 72–76, 93

Trinity, Trinitarian, 19, 25, 50–51,
   89, 93, 99–102, 108n12, 108n21,
   114n47, 114n48

victim, victimization, 4, 40–42, 45,
   48, 63, 87–88
victory, 1, 4, 14, 23, 24, 32, 46, 62, 82
violence, 2, 28, 37–38, 40–45, 49,
   55–57, 101, 103, 111n13, 119n1

water and spirit, 7, 73
Wink, Walter, 44